W9-CRO-804

Project
Text
for
Public
Speaking

Harper & Brothers

Publishers · New York

by CLARK S. CARLILE

Idaho State College

PROJECT TEXT FOR PUBLIC SPEAKING

Copyright, 1953, by Harper & Brothers
Printed in the United States of America

All rights in this book are reserved.
No part of the book may be used or reproduced
in any manner whatsoever without written per-
mission except in the case of brief quotations
embodied in critical articles and reviews. For
information address Harper & Brothers
49 East 33rd Street, New York 16, N.Y.

To

Professor James R. Start

Chairman of Speech Department
Ft. Hays Kansas State College, Hays, Kansas

A friend and former teacher

CONTENTS

CONTENTS (continued)

PREFACE

Learning to speak publicly is best accomplished by actual speaking experiences. Although it is desirable that a person possess some knowledge of what lies behind the act of public speaking, the important criterion of success is his ability to stand on his feet and demonstrate his power of speech. *It is the speech that counts;* hence this project text emphasizes actual speaking experiences. It is for the student who has to give a speech and who wants to know how to prepare and deliver it. *This book tells him how to do this* in simple, easy-to-understand language. The student has no need to ask his instructor time-consuming questions or to spend hours searching out information about a particular kind of speech. The information is in each assignment.

This text emphasizes the five basic purposes of public speaking: (1) to inform; (2) to stimulate; (3) to convince; (4) to entertain; (5) to get action. It stresses that a speaker must not only know his general purpose but that he must also state his specific purpose for every speech he presents.

The text is flexible in that it permits an instructor to select speaking experiences in any order and number that he sees fit for a quarter or a semester's work. Experience has shown it to be especially valuable in large classes divided into numerous sections. Here it permits unity and coherence of planning and ease of instruction, since every project consists of definite, complete, and specific information regarding that particular speech. The student knows exactly what is required for any speech. He must prepare a complete sentence outline; he must state his purpose; he must adhere to time limits. The instructor follows the outline during the speech, evaluates the speech on the outline itself, grades it, and returns it to the student at the end of the class period. Students thus have a record of their speeches and a written criticism of them.

Ease in teaching from this text may be achieved in a number of ways. A few suggestions follow:

1. Appoint a different student chairman for each class meeting. While the instructor takes the roll the chairman will gather all outlines, copy names and topics of all the speakers, arrange the outlines according to the order of speakers, hand the arranged outlines to the instructor, and then introduce the speakers in order. The instructor returns all outlines at the end of the session with comments and grades written on them.

2. All outlines should be ready when class convenes, or several days in advance if the instructor desires early preparation.

3. Students not wishing to tear outlines from their books may hand their texts to the instructor or chairman with the text open to the outline.

4. Appointing a student permanent timekeeper to give prearranged time signals and/or announce the time spoken is helpful.

5. The projects may be altered by: (1) assigning specific topics; (2) requiring use of a blackboard, charts, pictures, certain objects, or quotations in the speech; (3) requiring use of a specific type of introduction and/or conclusion, and changing speaking notes and time limit requirements.

6. Students may be required to memorize the criticism chart and thus be prepared to give immediate and detailed oral criticism in an organized manner.

7. Sources by interview, special observation, or written materials may be assigned.

8. Instructors may assign certain types of speeches to pairs of students, e.g., nomination and acceptance of a nomination, presenting a gift or award and accepting it, or a speech of welcome and a response to it.

At Idaho State College seven departmental staff members have used previous editions. Their comments have been invaluable. To Don Asboe, Mel Schubert, Carl Isaacson, Charlotte Cleeland, Charles Bilyeu, and Norma Cook thanks are in order. From Charles Bilyeu special help came in a suggestion improving the outline form. Dr. Vio M. Powell, department head, gave excellent support and encouragement. President Carl W. McIntosh, holder of a doctor's degree in speech and a former speech teacher, gladly gave his help.

Miss Lousene Rousseau, speech editor of Harper & Brothers Publishers, is extended particular recognition for her excellence and remarkable ability in suggesting desirable changes for improvement. Her advice was most helpful and valuable.

Patience, tolerant listening, and infinite charity were expressed at all times by my wife, who was my best critic and most valuable assistant.

Dozens of other persons have made contributions of merit, and gratitude to all is felt even though their names are not recorded here. One of these does deserve special recognition: Lona Grabert Campbell, a former student, who typed the manuscript. Her alertness and acumen led to numerous typographical corrections and improvements.

C. S. C.

February 7, 1953

STUDENT INFORMATION SURVEY

Fill in the following information chart.

Class. . . . . Section . . . . Date . . . .

Name . . . . Age. . . . . Sex . . . . Married . . . .

College address . . . . Year in college . . . .

Major Field . . . . Minor Field . . . .

Home address (not school address). *P. O. Box 223 . . . Las Altas* . . . .

Parents' names . . . .

Parents' occupation. . . . .

High school attended *Mtn. View High* . . . . . . Where . . . . When . *195* . . . .

Speech courses taken. . . . .

. . . .

Speeches given, and date . . . .

. . . .

Dramatic activities participated in . . . .

. . . .

Major interest in high school . . . .

. . . .

Known speech and/or hearing defects . . . .

. . . .

What I want to get from this course . . . .

. . . .

. . . .

Write below additional information you think will be helpful to your instructor (travel experience, military service, health, hobbies, places you have lived, etc.). Use the back of this page if necessary.

YOUR FIRST SPEECH

Your first speech gives you a chance to stand before your classmates and tell them something about yourself. You are not expected to give a long account of your life; by answering the questions at the end of this project you will introduce yourself to your audience (your classmates), and get the feel of standing on your feet and talking before a group of persons.

How to Prepare for Your First Talk

One reason for giving your first talk is to tell your audience enough concerning yourself so they will know something about you. In other words, they will get acquainted with you. Another purpose is to give you a chance to learn what it is like when many persons are sitting before you waiting to hear what you have to say. Some students get a thrill from it, others a scare. Actually the scare is only a feeling that comes to a speaker because certain glands in his body are functioning more than they usually do in a speech situation. Because people dislike this feeling they say they are scared. Instead of being scared of *speaking*, they are scared of a normal physical action that takes place within themselves. They associate this feeling with speech making, tie the two together, and say "speaking scares" them.

To be scared is normal. To be nervous is normal. To be tense is normal. You must experience these feelings; otherwise you will be as lifeless as an old shirt. These feelings are present in football players before and during a game. Great actors have them. Great speakers have them. Nervousness is the high-octane gas which provides these persons with the drive to give life to their performances. They need a normal amount of it because they use it. They *control* their nervousness (energy) and that is all you need to do. Do not try to rid yourself of nervousness entirely; you will gain control of this power. As you give more speeches throughout this course, you will discover your control growing stronger — and that is what you want.

Study the questions at the end of this project. Decide generally how you will answer them. It will help you to practice aloud several times, standing in front of a mirror while you speak. Do not memorize your answers word for word, because this will make them sound like a recitation. Copy the questions so that you can take them with you for use as notes.

How to Present Your First Speech

When your name is called walk quietly to the front of the room. Avoid "stomping" your feet, clicking your heels on the floor, or calling unnecessary attention to yourself. When you get there, stand on both feet. Do not place one foot forward, throw out your hip, and rest your weight on your rear foot in a bashful boy slouch. Keep your weight on both feet or on your slightly forward foot. An attitude of a soldier at attention or any similar stance is undesirable. Be alert and polite, and you may be sure that you will look all right.

Let your hands hang loosely at your sides unless you care to bring the one holding your notes up in front of you. It is certainly permissible to place a hand in your pocket or on the table top or chair back, if you do not call attention to the act. Hold your notes lightly between the thumb and index finger. Do not palm them, or roll, crumple, twist, or disfigure them in any way by continuous handling. When you refer to them, raise them high enough that you do not need to lower your head to glance at them.

If you feel like moving around a few paces, do so naturally, without shuffling or scraping your feet. When you are not changing your position, stand still and keep your feet quiet.

When you begin your speech, talk with your normal voice just as you would if you were telling a group of good friends about yourself. Good speaking is good conversation. Make an introductory statement. Show some interest in your remarks. Be sure that everyone can hear you. Look your audience directly in the eyes, but avoid a shifty, flitting type of gaze that never really stops anywhere. You may look at certain persons in different parts of the group, since you cannot very well look at everybody during the short time you are speaking.

When you are ready to end your remarks, conclude with a brief summarizing statement. Pause at least two seconds after your final words; then go easily and quietly to your seat. Do not rush, or crumple your notes into a wad and shove them in your pocket. On reaching your chair, avoid slouching down in it, sprawling out, heaving a big sigh, and in general going through a pantomime which says in effect, "Boy, I'm glad that's over!" You may feel that way; however, this is one time that advertising does not pay. Sit comfortably in your chair and remember that you are still giving an impression of yourself. If you have done your best, no one will complain.

BIBLIOGRAPHY[1]

Brigance, *Speech Comp.*, chap. 1.

Bryant & Wallace, *Fund.*, chap. 1.

Buehler, chaps. 1-3.

Dolman, chaps. 1, 2.

Murray, pp. 8-10.

Norvelle & Smith, chaps. 1,2.

O'Neill, chaps. 1-3.

Thompson, part 1.

Thonssen & Gilkinson, part 2.

Williamson, chap. 2.

NOTES FOR YOUR SPEECH

1. What shall we call you? Your name? Nickname? Where is your home?
2. What was the most frightful experience you ever had? Explain.
3. What was the most embarrassing experience you ever had? Explain.
4. What is your favorite food? Why?
5. What is your major interest in college?
6. Conclude with a summarizing statement about your future plans.

[1] Abbreviated bibliographies are given at the end of each project. For complete citations, see the master bibliography at the end of this book.

PROJECT 2

HOW TO PREPARE A SPEECH

You are to prepare a speech which will be presented to your class on a date assigned by your instructor. Follow the steps which are discussed below. As part of your preparation make a complete sentence outline of your speech. Use the form at the end of this project for your outline. Be ready to hand the outline to your instructor when he calls for it several days before you give your speech. You must have his approval of your outline before you present this particular speech.

Probably the worst and most frequent cause of poor speaking is lack of proper preparation. It is therefore of the utmost importance that you know how to go about preparing a speech. If you will make it a practice to prepare early and thoroughly you will probably never give a bad speech. By following the suggestions in this project you will learn how to prepare a speech that will bring you acclaim as well as satisfaction.

Sometimes a person is asked to speak on a specific subject to a specific audience. Other times he is asked to speak but is told nothing about his prospective audience nor is he requested to discuss any definite subject. Regardless of how little a person knows about the circumstances of his speech, in preparing it he should follow these steps according to his best judgment:

1. *Choose your subject on these bases:*
   A. Be sure you can find sufficient material on your subject so that you will be able to present a full and complete discussion of it.
   B. Be certain that your subject can be discussed successfully after you have narrowed it to fit your time limits.
   C. Decide whether your topic is *too technical, trivial, trite,* or *broad.* If it is any of these, alter it as necessary or find a new subject.
   D. Be sure your subject is appropriate to *you, your audience, the occasion,* and the *environment.* If your topic is not suitable to all these factors, do not use it.
   E. Allow yourself enough time for thorough preparation.
   F. Select a title that is provocative, brief, relevant to your subject, and interesting.
2. *Analyze your audience.* To adapt your speech to the people who will hear you, you must understand them. To analyze your audience, ask the following questions: How old are they? What are their occupations? Their social standing? Their education? Their religion? Their prejudices and beliefs? Their customs? Their economic status? What do they want from you?

   Some inquiry will be necessary to find the answers. However, once you know the type of people you will talk to, you can build your speech to fit their thinking and behavior. If your audience analysis is faulty your remarks may miss your hearers completely or leave them in a disappointed and confused state of mind. Careful audience analysis is one of the most important parts of preparing a speech.
3. *Decide on the purpose of your speech.* Make up your mind about what you want your audience to do after they have heard you speak. Do you want them to laugh, vote for a certain candidate, be aroused about traffic accidents, buy a car, or agree that fraternities should be abolished? Whatever you want from them is your purpose. Construct your entire speech so that the response you want will be forthcoming. Until your mind is firmly made up you will not be ready for the next step. *Decide now on the purpose.*
4. *Gather material for your speech.* Go to the library, locate sources, take notes on what you read, and list the information for every source called for on the back of the sample speech outline. Do the same if a person is your source of information.
5. The heart of your preparation is *organizing your material.* Set down the exact arrangement of the points you plan to discuss by dividing the speech into introduction, body, and conclusion. and preparing a complete sentence outline of the entire speech.

   A sample outline is given at the end of this project. Note that every statement is a complete simple sentence.

It is not necessary in the outline to observe the traditional requirement that there must be point B if there is an A, a main idea II if there is a I, etc. If you list supporting evidence under each main heading you will sometimes have only one item, sometimes two, three, four, or five items. You are not attempting to *divide* a main point or subpoint, but to list supporting evidence or ideas. No particular number of points is required; you need have only enough supporting evidence for any main point to make that point stick.

6. *Wording your speech* is the next step. Decide what language you will use when you expand your outline into the actual speech. Two general methods are recommended. You may write out your speech in full by following your outline to get the order of your points, then read it aloud several times until you know the order and arrangement well enough so that you can give the speech extemporaneously with a few speaker's notes or none at all. *Do not memorize it word for word* so that you can present it only one way. Every time you give it the words will be different but the ideas will be the same. However, introductions and conclusions are sometimes memorized fully or in part; this is permissible.

The second method for wording your speech is to *rehearse aloud* from your outline until you have attained definite mastery of the words you plan to use. Then construct a set of notes on a library card and rehearse aloud from them several times. Avoid word-for-word memorizing.

Sample of Speaker's Notes

Informative Speaking

1. World Needs Information

2. Spreads Information

3. Uses

   A. Business

   B. Education

   C. World Peace

4. Indispensable

While rehearsing, *do it aloud* and don't mumble. Stand in front of a mirror, gesture and move around when you feel like it, avoid memorizing favorite actions and gestures, be vigorous. Overdoing the presentation occasionally may help you get the feel of it. Practice until you have it the way you want it, be ready a day early, sleep on it the night before, approach it with a rested body and clear mind — and you will do better.

7. Formulate a *mental attitude* toward your speech and whatever nervousness you may have. A certain amount of tension is natural and good for you. Expect it. Don't worry about it — everybody gets nervous. Just remember that you will soon have it under control and that it will actually help you speak more effectively.

SAMPLE OUTLINE

Name. . . . . Date . . . . Type of speech . . *Informative* . . . .

Specific purpose of this speech . . . . . . *I want my audience to have a better understanding of the importance of informative speaking.* . . . . .No. of sources required . *3* . .

Sentence outline: 75-150 words.   Time limit: 4-5 minutes.   Speaking notes: None.

TITLE   The Role of the Informative Speech

INTRODUCTION
    I. The world is constantly seeking information.
       A. Information promotes progress and understanding.
         1. Information is basic to both.

BODY
    I. Speech making quickly spreads information.
       A. The informative speech is important.
         1. Special information can be presented.
         2. General information can be offered.
         3. Information can be made interesting.
            a. Humor livens up informative speaking.
            b. Visual aids are a helpful means.
       B. Informative speaking can be used many ways.
         1. Business employs informative speeches.
         2. Education relies on informative speaking.
         3. World peace depends on informative talk.

CONCLUSION
    I. The role of informative speaking is indispensable.
       A. No type of speech can replace it.
       B. No type of speech is more significant.

SOURCES OF INFORMATION
    Baird, A. Craig, and Knower, Franklin H., *General Speech, an Introduction,*
       McGraw-Hill Book Company, Inc., 1949, Chapter 18.
    Oliver, Robert T., and Cortright, Rupert L., *New Training for Effective Speech,*
       rev. ed., The Dryden Press, 1950, Chapter 16.
    Soper, Paul L., *Basic Public Speaking,* Oxford University Press, 1949, pages 38-40.

BIBLIOGRAPHY

Borchers & Wise, chaps. 8, 9.
Brigance, *Speech Comm.*, chaps. 3-7.
Brigance, *Speech Comp.*, chaps. 1-6.
Brigance & Immel, chaps. 11-20.
Bryant & Wallace, *Fund.*, chaps. 5-12, 16-21.
Crocker, *Pub. Spkg.*, chaps. 6-21.
Dolman, chaps. 2-12.
Glasgow, chap. 4.
Gray & Braden, chaps. 2, 5, 7, 19.
Hibbitt, chaps. 5, 6.

Murray, chap. 5.
Norvelle & Smith, chaps. 1-10.
O'Neill, chaps. 4-8, 10, 11.
O'Neill & Weaver, chaps. 12-16.
Sandford & Yeager, *Prac. Bus. Spkg.*, chaps. 2-7.
Thonssen & Gilkinson, chaps. 13-20.
Thonssen & Scanlan, chaps. 2-9.
Williamson, chaps. 9-15.
Winans, chaps. 3-10.
Wise & others, chap. 14.

Name . . . . Date . . . . Type of speech . . . .

Specific purpose of this speech . . . .

. . . . No. of sources required . . . .

Sentence outline: 75-150 words. Time limit: 2-4 minutes. Speaking notes: 10-word limit.

TITLE

INTRODUCTION

.BODY

CONCLUSION

INSTRUCTOR'S COMMENTS

Clarity of purpose. . . . .

Gesture-action-eye contact . . . .

Language . . . .

Voice . . . .

Enthusiasm and vigor . . . .

Self-confidence . . . .

Organization . . . .

Introduction and conclusion . . . .

Grade. . . . .

(List sources on back of page as indicated)

PRINTED SOURCES OF INFORMATION

Give complete information for each source.

1. Author's name ....
   Title of article...
   Book or magazine containing article ....
   .... Date of publication ....
   Chapters and/or pages containing material ....

2. Author's name ....
   Title of article...
   Book or magazine containing article ....
   .... Date of publication...............
   Chapters and/or pages containing material ....

3. Author's name ....
   Title of article...
   Book or magazine containing article ....
   .... Date of publication ....
   Chapters and/or pages containing material ....

INTERVIEW SOURCES OF INFORMATION

1. Name of person interviewed .... Date of interview ....
   His title, position, and occupation ....
   ....
   Why is he an authority on the subject? Be specific ....
   ....

2. Name of person interviewed .... Date of interview ....
   His title, position, and occupation ....
   ....
   Why is he an authority on the subject? Be specific ....
   ....

3. Name of person interviewed .... Date of interview ....
   His title, position, and occupation ....
   ....
   Why is he an authority on the subject? Be specific ....
   ....

THE INTRODUCTION – BEGINNING A SPEECH

Prepare three different kinds of introductions, using the types listed below as guides. Unless your instructor designates otherwise, use only one subject, i.e., *Alaska*, which you will introduce in three different ways.

Speakers often fail to realize that the first words they utter may be their most important. Some trust to luck that they will be able to get started when they begin speaking. Always plan carefully the introduction of your speech; otherwise you are more than likely to have an awkward, poorly organized, and haphazard introduction which will make your audience uneasy and cause them to lose whatever interest and confidence they may have felt in you and your subject.

Explanation of the Introduction

1. One purpose of the introduction is to *gain the attention, arouse the interest,* or *excite the curiosity* of listeners. This may be done in numerous ways.
    A. *Refer to the occasion and purpose of the meeting* with a few brief remarks explaining and commenting on why the audience has gathered, or refer to special interests of the audience and show how your subject is connected with these interests.
    B. *Pay the audience a genuine compliment* on their hospitality, their interest in the subject to be discussed, their concern over bettering their community, their progressive educational program, the outstanding leadership of the group sponsoring the speech. The sincerity of the speaker should be genuine, since the audience's judgment of his speech will be strongly influenced by his opening phrases.
    C. *Tell a story* (human interest, humorous, exciting, etc.) that catches attention and arouses curiosity. *Link the story to your subject.* If it is not related to the subject, don't tell it.
    D. *Refer to a recent incident* the audience is acquainted with.
    E. *Use a quotation* to open your remarks and set the stage for the subject. The quotation should be relevant, and be tied to your thoughts with a few brief explanations. Do not prolong this type of introduction.
    F. *Use a novel idea or a striking statement* to arouse curiosity and interest or to gain attention. This should not be overdone. If it is sheer sensationalism it will lose its punch because the remainder of the speech cannot be so shocking.
    G. *Refer to a preceding speaker* and his thoughts in order to secure interest and attention. However, do not give this too much elaboration.
    H. *Put pertinent and challenging questions* to the audience to arouse their curiosity — "Do you know the cost of ...? Do you want your government to ...? Are you willing to stand around while ...?"
    Various combinations of the above suggestions may provide an effective introduction.
2. A second purpose of the introduction may be *to prepare and open the minds of the hearers for the thoughts which are to come.* This is particularly necessary if the audience is hostile. It may be accomplished by giving background and historical information so that the audience can and will understand the subject. It may be further achieved if the speaker establishes his right to speak by recounting the research he has done on his subject, by naming prominent persons associated with him in his endeavor, and by telling modestly about certain honors, offices, and awards he has received as the result of his accomplishments in fields closely related to his topic.
3. A third objective of the introduction may be *to indicate the purpose of the speech.* This may be achieved by stating the subject generally and explaining the thesis of the talk. A bare statement of the topic is not enough — it is uninteresting and in most cases dull. An appropriate and interesting exposition should be given any general statement of the subject.

Suggested Introductions

If you have trouble finding a subject to introduce, look at the suggested topics for speeches listed in other projects in this book. If you wish, you may ask permission to prepare the assignment on introductions and conclusions jointly, using one subject for both.

How to Prepare an Introduction

When you prepare your introduction, keep in mind the fact that what you prepare is to pave the way for what is to come later in your speech. However, it often happens that when the chairman introduces you he says something that forces you to alter your opening remarks. It may be that the environment will prompt you to remark about it, or some incident occurring in the audience may require comment. Whatever the circumstances, be prepared to speak impromptu as you feel the occasion demands, then begin your planned introduction by making an easy transition to it.

Your introduction should be built around the purpose you want it to achieve. You alone must decide what this purpose will be. Adapt your introduction to the expected audience, the occasion, and the environment. Be sure also that it is adapted to you, your prestige, and your position in the eyes of your listeners.

Your wording should be carefully worked out. Rehearse your introduction at least four or five times to fix it well in mind. It should not be memorized word for word, although the ideas you wish to present should be memorized in their proper sequence.

The introduction to a speech is often prepared last, because it can thus be built around the final draft of the speech. If it were prepared first it might not merge with and be appropriate to the body of the speech. Also, its length can be determined more advantageously. Ordinarily it will consume no more than one quarter of the total time, and often it will be much less.

There are a few points to remember when preparing your introduction. Avoid dullness and triteness, undue length of opening remarks, false leads that are not followed up, stories which are suggestive or risque or used only to fill time, or a mere announcement of the topic. Avoid apologies or remarks which might be construed as apologies. Try to devise a fresh and original approach that will set the stage for what is to come later in your speech and at the same time bring you and your audience together in a friendly atmosphere.

How to Present an Introduction

An important aspect of the introduction is the speaker's behavior before he takes the platform and after he gets there. If he is sitting on stage in full view of his audience he should remain comfortably and calmly alert. People are appraising him while he waits. Women speakers should be careful not to cross their knees while seated. Crossing the ankles is permissable, although it is safer to keep both feet on the floor with the knees together. When the speaker is introduced he should rise easily without delay or noise and move to his place on the platform. After arriving, a few seconds should elapse while he deliberately surveys the scene before him. Then, after addressing the chairman, if he has not already done so, he is ready to begin his introductory remarks.

He should speak clearly, distinctly, and loudly enough to be heard easily by all present. It is best to begin somewhat slowly, then speed up the rate later.

BIBLIOGRAPHY

Brigance, *Speech Comp.*, pp. 67-85.
Brigance & Immel, pp. 363-369.
Bryant & Wallace, *Fund.*, pp. 248-260.
Crocker, *Pub. Spkg.*, pp. 188-198.
Glasgow, pp. 74-80.
Gray & Braden, chap. 13.
Monroe, *Prin. & Types*, pp. 194-199.
Norvelle & Smith, chap. 6.
Oliver & Cortright, pp. 167-169.
O'Neill, pp. 294-301.
Parrish, *Spkg. in Pub.*, pp. 155-162.

Powers, pp. 175-178.
Runion, pp. 58-65.
Sandford & Yeager, *Prac. Bus. Spkg.*, pp. 80-81, 117-118.
Sandford & Yeager, *Prin.*, chap. 11.
Sarett & Foster, pp. 384-420.
Schubert, pp. 138-139.
Thompson, pp. 26-28.
Thonssen & Gilkinson, pp. 285-290.
Weaver, pp. 90-94.
Williamson & others, pp. 223, 236.

Examples of Introductions

Baird, *Repres. Amer. Speeches*, 1949-50, pp. 67, 142, 164, 231; *ibid.*, 1950-51, pp. 14, 46, 84, 118, 131, 141, 150.
Vital Speeches of the Day, any recent issue.

Name . . . . Date . . . .

Outline: Prepare a 15-30-word complete sentence outline for three different introductions. Hand these to your instructor when you are asked to speak.

Time limit: 1-2 minutes for each introduction.

Speaking notes: None.

First Introduction: What kind?

Second Introduction: What kind?

(over)

Third Introduction: What kind?

INSTRUCTOR'S COMMENTS

Grade . . . .

PROJECT 4

THE CONCLUSION – ENDING A SPEECH

Prepare three different kinds of conclusions, using the types listed below as guides. Unless your instructor designates otherwise, use only one subject, i.e., *crime;* you will prepare three conclusions to an imagined speech on the subject.

No doubt you have often heard a speaker stop suddenly, leaving you with a feeling of being dangled in mid air. You may have wondered why he stopped there or you may have wanted him to pull his remarks together so you could grasp his thoughts in their fullness. You have surely also heard a speaker pass a half dozen stop signs, any one of which should have been his conclusion. Either type of conclusion is poor, and represents careless planning.

By working out separate conclusions which demonstrate in themselves various methods of ending a speech, you not only learn how to do them but you become aware of one of the most important parts of every speech, the conclusion.

Explanation of the Conclusion

The conclusion brings together all the thoughts, emotions, discussions, arguments, and feelings which the speaker has tried to communicate to his audience. In an impressive speech the closing words should make a powerful emotional impression on the listeners, because in most cases logic alone is insufficient to move an audience to act or believe as the speaker suggests. Furthermore, the conclusion is the last opportunity to emphasize the point of a speech. It should be a natural culmination of all that has been said. It should not be weak and insipid, begun or ended just as the speaker starts on his hesitating journey toward his chair.

There are numerous ways to develop a conclusion. Some of the better known are the following:

1. A *summary* is sometimes used. This may be expressed by restatement of the speech title, the purpose, or a specific phrase that has been used several times in the speech, by an apt quotation, either prose or poetry, that adroitly says what the speaker wants said, or by any other means that tends to bring the main point of the speech into final focus for the audience.

2. *Recapitulation* may be used in longer formal speeches when it is necessary to restate points in a 1-2-3 order. The danger here is that it may become monotonous and uninteresting. Short speeches do not require this type of conclusion, because the points are easily remembered. A short speech may close with the last main point if it is a strong point. Usually, however, more is needed to close a speech, even a short one.

3. A striking *anecdote, analogy,* or *simile* may be employed as a closing remark, or any one of them or a suitable combination of them may be interwoven with the summary or recapitulation type of conclusion.

4. *An emotionalized or idealized statement of the thesis* may serve as a useful conclusion.

5. *The thesis may be powerfully restated.*

6. *A vivid illustration of the central idea* may conclude a speech fittingly.

7. *A call for action from the audience* may end a speech. It must of course pertain to the ideas of the speaker. This is an excellent type of conclusion, particularly when the purpose has been to stimulate or to get action from the audience.

How to Prepare a Conclusion

The conclusion should always be one of the most carefully prepared parts of a speech. Just when it should be prepared is largely a matter of opinion. Some authorities advise preparing it first because this practice enables a speaker to point his talk toward a predetermined end. Others suggest preparing the conclusion last because this procedure allows one to draw his final words from the full draft of his speech. Regardless of when the conclusion is prepared, there is one point on which all authorities agree: the conclusion must be carefully worded, carefully organized, carefully rehearsed, and in most cases committed to memory or nearly so. The conclusion should be brief, generally not more than one-eighth to one-tenth of the entire speech, and perhaps less, depending on the speech, the speaker, the audience, the occasion, and the environment in which the speech is delivered. A conclusion should never bring in new material, for this creates an undesirable anticlimax and frequently irritates an audience because the speaker runs past a perfect place to stop.

When preparing your conclusion you will find no formula that tells which type is best for a given speech. Your own judgment and a critical evaluation of what you want your conclusion to do are the only means for selecting the particular kind you will use. However, since the conclusion is so important, weigh the advantages and adaptability of all of them before making your decision.

How to Present a Conclusion

The importance of the delivery of a conclusion cannot be overemphasized. Your total organism — mind, body, and soul — must be harmoniously at work. Eye contact should be direct, gestures and actions appropriate, posture alert, and the voice sincere, distinct, and well articulated. When you move into your conclusion, it should be obvious that you are closing your remarks. Your intentions should be so clear that you should not have to tell the audience what you are doing by saying, "In conclusion . . ."

One final word of warning. When the speech is finished, hold the floor for a second or two (this cannot be stressed enough), then return to your chair and seat yourself quietly. Display or frivolity of any kind after the speech may sharply alter many good impressions made while on the platform.

BIBLIOGRAPHY

Brigance, *Speech Comp.*, pp. 109, 118.
Brigance & Immel, pp. 369-375.
Bryant & Wallace, *Fund.*, pp. 261-262.
Crocker, *Pub. Spkg.*, pp. 214-218.
Glasgow, pp. 94-96.
Gray & Braden, chap. 15.
Monroe, *Prin. & Types*, pp. 208-212.
Norvelle & Smith, chap. 10.
Oliver & Cortright, pp. 169-173.
O'Neill, pp. 304-307.

Parrish, *Spkg. in Pub.*, pp. 170-173.
Sandford & Yeager, *Prac. Bus. Spkg.*, pp. 81, 105-106, 117-118.
Sandford & Yeager, *Prin.*, chap. 11.
Sarett & Foster, pp. 510-524.
Schubert, pp. 144-145.
Thompson, pp. 29-30.
Thonssen & Gilkinson, pp. 293-295.
Weaver, pp. 96-98.
Williamson, chap. 14.
Williamson & others, pp. 236-243.

Examples of Conclusions

Baird, *Rep. Amer. Speeches*, 1949-50, pp. 27, 36, 84, 94, 99, 116, 126, 158, 211, 229; *ibid.*, 1950-51, pp. 36, 52, 70, 92, 148.
Vital Speeches of the Day, any recent issue.

Name . . . . Date . . . .

Outline: Prepare a 15-30-word complete sentence outline for three different conclusions. Hand these to your instructor when you are asked to speak.

Time limit: 1/2 to 2 minutes for each conclusion.

Speaking notes: None.

First Conclusion: What kind?

Second Conclusion: What kind?

(Over)

Third Conclusion: What kind?

INSTRUCTOR'S COMMENTS:

Grade . . . .

RECORDING A SPEECH

Time limit: To be assigned.
Speaking notes: 10 or 15 words should be enough.

This project gives you a chance to hear and judge your own speaking. It calls for a speech that you will record and keep for yourself to show how you talked when this course started. At a later date near the end of the course you may wish to make another recording to compare with your first recording, thus noting your progress.

A recorded speech may be any kind for any occasion. It is simply a speech that is recorded and played back at will. In other words, it becomes a record in voice rather than a record in writing. Its special feature is the time limit placed on the speaker. The time has to be observed within a matter of seconds. Any person who is not willing to adhere to the time limit pays for disk space he does not use if his speech is short or makes an awkward conclusion or is cut off in the middle of a sentence or summary if it is too long.

Suggested Topics for Recording

If you are recording a speech during the first part of the school year with the thought in mind that you will make a later recording for purposes of comparison, it may be wise to use the first speech experience suggested in this book, the one in which you introduced yourself to the class. If you do not care to do this, check through the many possibilities listed under "Suggested Topics" in the other projects. Be sure your selection meets the time limit which you will be required to observe. Consult your instructor for further information. Do not try to be profound in your remarks. Rather, select a topic which will best represent you at your present stage of development as a speaker.

How to Prepare a Speech for Recording

In this particular speech your purpose is to secure a record of your speaking ability. In accordance with the speaker's notes in Project 1, decide what you are going to say; then practice aloud until you have your thoughts well in mind, but not memorized. Know the general outline of your ideas. If you choose some other topic, prepare it as you would any speech by observing good speech preparation practices. In all cases observe your time limit within ten seconds if possible.

Should you choose to read your speech (with your instructor's consent), organize it as you would any speech. Keep it right on the nose as to time.

How to Present a Speech for Recording

Begin your speech by saying, "This is (George Jones) speaking on (date)..." After this first sentence, go ahead with your talk. Speak in your natural voice as you normally would. Be careful not to vary the distance from the microphone by moving your head a great deal, or your recording may be loud at first and then weak. Avoid coughing, clearing your throat, sneezing, and shouting into the "mike." Ask your instructor how close to stand to the microphone; ten inches is usually a good distance.

While speaking, watch your progress so that you will be sure to finish before your time runs out. If you use notes, avoid rustling them near the microphone. Any sound they make will be picked up and exaggerated. When you are through with one piece of paper, let it fall quietly from your hands to the floor.

Special Notes

If disks are used for recordings, the following may apply. When a group of recordings is concluded, the instructor may play them back to the class and members of the class may then discuss the individual speakers. Points to listen for are the whistled "s," nasality, harshness, resonance, pitch, force, articulation, pronunciation, rate, sentence structure, diction, vocabulary, and grammar.

The instructor at his discretion may keep the records on file until the end of the course when final recordings may be made for comparative purposes. The student may then be given a record with a speech on each side for his own use and analysis.

Blank disks may be procured from a local music store or the instructor may write to the various record-making companies for them. He should ask for educational discounts, regardless of where he gets them. Each student should be prepared to pay for the disk used for his recording unless the school provides for this expense. If a wire or tape recorder is used, there will be no expense unless the spool is retained for future reference, in which case another spool will be needed to replace it. Even in this case, the used spool may be filed until near the end of the term at which time it can be reused without cost.

BIBLIOGRAPHY

Hibbitt, pp. 289-291.

PROJECT 6

THE PERSONAL EXPERIENCE SPEECH

You take a step forward in your speaking experience when you present a personal experience speech. Although this speech is essentially about yourself, it still requires definite preparation and interesting presentation. You should learn the importance of these two requirements early in your speech training. Aside from becoming acquainted with these aspects of speech making, you should feel increased confidence and poise as a result of this speech experience. Your ease before the group will improve noticeably. By giving your best to this speech you will achieve creditable improvement and a desirable personal satisfaction.

Explanation of a Personal Experience Speech

Determine the specific purpose of your remarks. If you want to tell about funny or amusing personal experiences, you will plan to *entertain* your listeners. If you want to tell how you trap muskrats, your purpose will be to *inform* your listeners. It is advisable to confine your efforts to one of these two kinds of speeches. Study the particular project in this book that deals with the type of speech you plan to present.

Suggested Topics for a Personal Experience Speech

1. A car wreck.	8. Climbing a mountain.	15. An interesting job.
2. The big fire.	9. Racing—any kind.	16. Wrestling—professional.
3. Falling through ice.	10. Sailing a boat.	17. Carnival rackets.
4. Nearly drowning.	11. My first rodeo.	18. A ski contest.
5. Big game.	12. A robbery.	19. A great book.
6. In the Army.	13. Learning to fly.	20. Building something.
7. Aboard a ship.	14. A chemical experiment.	21. Speaker's choice.

Do not choose a trip unless you have more to tell about than such items as the time you started, where you ate, the hotels you stayed in, the cities you passed through, and when you returned. A speech of this kind should have some element of *special* interest which makes it different from any ordinary trip.

How to Choose a Topic for a Personal Experience Speech

Read the foregoing list of topics carefully. If you have had an exciting experience suggested by one of them, select it for your speech. Whatever you decide to talk about should be vivid in your memory. When you think about it you may feel prickly chills race up your spine, you may feel sad. But whatever it is, the experience should be personal.

Do not begin to stall about choosing a topic because you do not know anything interesting to talk about. This is an old worn-out excuse which explorers used before Columbus; they could not make up their minds about what to discover. In all likelihood they did not try. The topic you choose will not be interesting in itself. It is your responsibility to plan to tell the personal experience in an interesting way. You can do this with a little effort. Choose a topic without delay, and then read the rest of this project to find out how to prepare and present a speech on such a topic.

How to Prepare a Personal Experience Speech

Let us assume that you know generally what is expected of you when you give your speech. Let us assume, too, that you have your purpose constantly before you (to entertain or to inform). Now develop your speech in the following order:

1. Outline your speech in considerable detail. This means that you must set up the order of the events you want to talk about. Be sure your outline places these events in their most effective order throughout your talk. A little thought about arrangement will tell you how to place your ideas. In arranging what you will talk about, include your own personal feelings and reactions, the activities of other persons or animals, and objects that made your experience thrilling, exciting, or funny. This will add interest.

2. Practice your speech aloud before friends and in front of a mirror. Do this until you have memorized the sequence of events, *not the words*. You will naturally tend to memorize certain words and phrases and this is all right. But do not under any circumstances memorize the whole speech word for word. Every time you rehearse you will tell the same things, but never with exactly the same words. Each rehearsal will set the pattern of your speech more firmly in mind until after several practices (the number depends on the individual) you will be able to present your speech with full confidence and the knowledge that you know what you are going to say; that is, you know the events and feelings you are going to talk about and describe.

3. Make a final evaluation of your speech before marking it "ready for presentation." Ask yourself the following questions and be sure that your speech answers each question adequately.

   A. Does your speech merely list a series of persons, places, and things without telling what happened to these persons and things? (Vitalize these persons and things by describing what happened and by pointing out unusual or exciting incidents, such as dangers or humorous occurrences.) Avoid unnecessary details.

   B. Is your speech about *you only*? If so, you can improve it by talking about the influences that were operating in your presence. For example, if you rescued a drowning person, do not be satisfied to say, "I jumped in and pulled him out." Tell what he was doing, describe his struggles, tell how deep the water was, how far he was from shore, recount your fears and other feelings as you pulled him toward shore, tell how the current almost took you under, demonstrate the way you held him by the hair. Emphasize such items as your fatigue and near-exhaustion as you fought to stay afloat.

   C. Do you have a curiosity-arousing introduction, one that catches the attention?

   D. Do you have a conclusion? A speech is never finished without one.

How to Present a Personal Experience Speech

Your attitude regarding yourself and your audience will exert marked influence upon you and your listeners. You should have a sincere desire to entertain or inform. If it is information that you earnestly desire to give, try to make your audience understand what you are telling. If it is entertainment that you want to provide, strive to give enjoyment by amusing and causing smiles and perhaps some laughter. You should not feel that what you have to say is simply not interesting and never was, which is the attitude some students have. Consider for a moment the child who runs eagerly, grasps your hand, and excitedly tells you about a big dog two doors down the street. His story no doubt captures your interest; yet there is nothing inherently interesting about a big dog you have seen many times. Why then are you interested? The answer lies largely in the extreme desire of the child to tell you something. *He wants you to understand him,* and therein lies the basic secret of giving information to which people will listen attentively. You must have a desire to make your audience understand you and enjoy what you are saying.

As for bodily actions and gestures, demonstrate the points you can. Let your arms and hands gesture whenever you feel an impulse to do so; otherwise, your hands may hang comfortably at your sides, rest easily on a table top or chair back, or be placed conveniently in a pocket. Be calm about putting your hands anywhere. Feel free to change your stage position by moving laterally a few feet. This will cause attention to be drawn to your presentation.

Use your voice normally and conversationally. Talk earnestly and loudly enough to be heard by everyone present. If you are truly interested in your audience's understanding you, your voice modulation and force will take care of themselves very well.

If you use speaking notes, observe the ten-word maximum. Have them in large handwriting so that they can be read easily. Use a paper or card at least three by five inches in size. When referring to your notes, *raise them* to a level that permits you to glance at them without bowing your head. Do not try to hide them, nor act ashamed of using them. They are your map.

BIBLIOGRAPHY

Bryant & Wallace, *Fund.*, chap. 2.
Buehler, part 1, chaps. 4, 5.
Crocker, *Pub. Spkg.*, chap. 1.
Dolman, chaps. 1-5.

Hibbitt, chap. 5.
O'Neill, chaps. 4-6.
Thompson, parts 1, 2.
Thonssen & Gilkinson, chap. 14.

SPEECH OUTLINE, PROJECT 6

Name . . . . Date . . . . Type of speech . . . .

Specific purpose of this speech . . . .

. . . .

Sentence outline: 50-100 words   Time limit: 3-4 minutes   Speaking notes: 10-word limit.

TITLE

INTRODUCTION

BODY

CONCLUSION

INSTRUCTOR'S COMMENTS

   Clarity of purpose . . . .

   Gesture-action-eye contact . . . .

   Language . . . .

   Voice . . . .

   Enthusiasm and vigor . . . .

   Self-confidence . . . .

   Organization . . . .

   Introduction and conclusion . . . .

   Grade . . . .

(List sources on back of page as indicated)

PRINTED SOURCES OF INFORMATION

Give complete information for each source.

1. Author's name . . . .

   Title of article. . . . .

   Book or magazine containing article . . . .

   . . . . Date of publication . . . .

   Chapters and/or pages containing material. . . . .

2. Author's name . . . .

   Title of article. . . . .

   Book or magazine containing article . . . .

   . . . . Date of publication . . . .

   Chapters and/or pages containing material . . . .

3. Author's name . . . .

   Title of article. . . . .

   Book or magazine containing article . . . .

   . . . . Date of publication . . . .

INTERVIEW SOURCES OF INFORMATION

1. Name of person interviewed. . . . . Date of interview . . . .

   His title, position, and occupation . . . .

   . . . .

   Why is he an authority on the subject? Be specific. . . . .

   . . . .

2. Name of person interviewed. . . . . .Date of interview . . . .

   His title, position, and occupation . . . .

   . . . .

   Why is he an authority on the subject? Be specific . . . .

   . . . .

3. Name of person interviewed . . . . Date of interview . . . .

   His title, position, and occupation . . . .

   . . . .

   Why is he an authority on the subject? Be specific. . . . .

   . . . .

THE PET PEEVE SPEECH

Time limit: None.
Speaking notes: Do as you like; you will probably be more effective without them.
Source of information: Yourself.
Outline of speech: None required.

Thus far in your speeches you have probably felt varying degrees of nervousness and tension. As a result you may have taken the stage fearfully, spoken in hushed weak tones, used little or no bodily action and scarcely any gestures. Perhaps you have not looked your audience in the eye (eye contact) or you may have lacked sufficient enthusiasm. Such behavior on your part is probably caused by thinking of yourself and how you are doing.

One way to overcome tension and nervousness is to talk about something that arouses you intensely. This speech is designed to give you the feeling of real, live speaking in which you cast aside all inhibitions, fears, and thoughts of yourself. See what you can do with it.

Explanation of the Pet Peeve Speech

Your talk should be about your own pet peeve. It should concern your innermost feelings on the peeve which arouses in you greater disturbance and anger or feeling than anything else. It should make your blood boil just to think of it. It may be about something of recent occurrence or it may concern an event that happened some time ago. It must, however, be about an incident that is vivid in your memory. Probably it should be of recent date; otherwise, you may have cooled off too much to make a strong speech about it.

How to Prepare a Speech About a Pet Peeve

No particular preparation is required. All you need do is to decide what your most annoying and irritating pet peeve is. Once you make your choice, mull over the irritating idea and make up your mind that you are going to "blow off a lot of steam" to your audience. If you wish to rehearse before presentation, so much the better. However, for this specific assignment you are not asked to practice. All that you are asked to do is to make sure that you are "red hot" about a particular subject. *If you are,* your preparation is sufficient for this speech.

How to Present Your Speech

There is just one way to deliver a speech about a pet peeve. Put your whole body and soul into it. Mean every word. Use plenty of force and colorful language. Let a slow fire that has been smoldering within you suddenly blaze up. In other words, let yourself go as never before. Quit pussyfooting around and acting like a meek little lamb that has lost its way. Be a man for a change and let the world know it. If your arms feel like waving, let them wave. If you feel like scowling, scowl. If you feel like shouting, shout. Whatever you do, be sure you go all out. No doubt you will be surprised at your own ability -- when you really "unload" your pet peeve.

After your speech, the instructor and class will comment orally on your effectiveness. They should be able to tell you whether or not you really meant what you said. It will be helpful to you to find out how they reacted.

BIBLIOGRAPHY

Brigance, *Speech Comp.*, chaps. 2,3.
Brigance, *Spoken Word*, chaps. 1-4.
Bryant & Wallace, *Oral Comm.*, chap. 2.
Dolman, chaps. 1-5.

Monroe, *Prin. & Types*, chap. 1.
Monroe, *Prin. of Speech*, chap. 1.
O'Neill, chaps. 8,9.
Thompson, parts 1,2.

PROJECT 8

THE BODILY ACTION AND GESTURE SPEECH

Speaking is a total bodily activity. To be really effective a person has to talk all over. He has to use his feet and legs, his hands and arms, his trunk, his head, his eyebrows -- every part of him. Many beginning speakers do not realize this, despite the fact that they themselves use total bodily expression all the time in their normal conversation. One sees such speakers standing rigidly before a class when they make their speeches. They move only their vocal chords, their soft palates, tongues, and jaws. Actually they are half speaking (communicating) because they are using only half of their communicating tools. If they would put *all* their speaking power into action, they would include bodily action and gestures. A speech project of this kind is included because it provides an experience which demands that the speaker use bodily actions and gestures and thus improve his speech.

Explanation of Bodily Action and Gestures in Speech

A speech to illustrate bodily activity may be of any kind, since bodily actions and gestures should be used with varying degree in every speech. The purpose of your speech need not be influenced because bodily actions and gestures are required. These activities will assist you to communicate in a manner which fulfills your purpose, regardless of what it is.

Bodily actions may be defined as movements of the body as it changes place. Gestures may be defined as movements of individual parts of the body, such as raising an eyebrow, shrugging the shoulders, pointing.

This speech in which you deliberately use bodily actions and gestures should be considered as an experience in which you *plan* to utilize your entire organism and *then do it.* This will make you understand how much more effective you really are and thus set a pattern of speaking to be used in future speeches.

Actually, it is impossible to speak without some bodily actions and gestures. The fact that you may not be aware of all that goes on while you speak in no sense means that you are not using *some* actions. Your very nervousness and stage fright elicit certain gestures which tell your audience that you are nervous. Now, if you substitute *meaningful* activity, you at once improve your communication and release many nervous tensions which accompany speaking. The point to bear in mind is that all speech communication should be accompanied by *appropriate* and *meaningful* bodily actions and gestures; this should not be interpreted to mean that you must constantly employ bodily movements and gestures. Such monotony of motion would be nerve wracking to an audience. If moderation is good to practice in all things, this holds true of total bodily expression. Keep this in mind.

Suggested Topics for Bodily Action and Gesture Speeches

1. How to use a baseball bat properly -- demonstrate with bat.
2. How to catch and throw a football.
3. How to dribble and "shoot" a basketball.
4. How to box -- demonstrate.
5. How to use judo.
6. How to fly a model airplane.
7. How to revive a drowning person.
8. How to apply a tourniquet.
9. How to cast when fly fishing.
10. How to shoot a gun (pistol, rifle, shotgun).
11. How to walk properly.
12. How to model clothes.
13. How to drive a car and use the proper hand signals.
14. How to dance. (Different steps should be demonstrated and explained. Also different types of dancing such as square, tap, ballet.)

15. How to paddle a canoe.
16. How to ice skate or roller skate.
17. How to construct something.
18. How to do card tricks. (This must be a demonstration which uses bodily action and gestures — not the mere performance of a few tricks.)
19. How to ski, toboggan.
20. Speaker's choice.

How to Choose a Topic for a Bodily Action and Gesture Speech

Since the purpose of presenting this speech is to improve your use of bodily action and gesture, select a subject which you can demonstrate while talking about it. On the other hand, since the purpose of the speech itself is to inform your listeners, choose a topic that you are both interested in and informed about.

Study the above list carefully. Any of these topics can be made suitable for your audience by your skill in explaining or demonstrating. After your choice is made, stick to it even if you discover that it is more difficult to prepare than you had anticipated. Do not change your topic just because you misjudged the amount of effort it would take for preparation. It is important that you select a topic without delay, for this speech will require considerable planning.

How to Prepare a Bodily Action and Gesture Speech

In the speech to develop bodily action and gesture, your *communicative purpose* is to inform your listeners in such a way that they understand what you are talking about. Read the material in Project 12, "The Speech to Inform — Any Subject." Develop your speech in the manner suggested for the informative speech.

In rehearsing, you will need to practice bodily actions and gestures, for these will constitute the major part of this speech. The actions should not be memorized in detail, for this will result in a mechanical performance on your part. Instead, stand before a mirror while you practice -- if possible, a full-length mirror. However, if only a small mirror is available, do the best you can with it. A friend who will watch you and give helpful criticisms provides an excellent means for improvement.

While you rehearse, make an effort to create a well-organized set of spontaneous actions. As stated above, do not memorize these actions. They must be motivated by the earnestness of your desire to make your hearers understand you. You must feel impelled to use your body and hands in expressing yourself. These actions of your body and hands need not be like those of anybody else; they are your own, the same as your walk and style of dancing are your own. All that you need to do is observe yourself when practicing in order to eliminate awkwardness, undesirable posture, and distracting mannerisms.

If you are willing to undergo a little self-inflicted criticism, you can develop your own style of gesture and bodily action. In doing this, it is advisable that you read several of the references at the end of this project.

Your posture should be one of alertness in which you *stand tall.* Keep your weight on the balls of your feet and on the forward foot. Bodily action should be free, relaxed, easy. It should have tonicity, vigor, and coordination, without the appearance of extreme nervous tension, which is characterized by shuffling feet and restless tiger-like pacing. In moving to the left, lead with the left foot; to the right, with the right foot. Avoid crossing your feet in order to get started. Move quietly without "clomping" heels and scraping soles. Be sure that the movement is motivated and acts as a transition between ideas, as an emphasis, as a device for releasing bodily tension and for holding attention. Use bodily action deliberately until you habitually make it a desirable part of your speech, a part that communicates meanings and ideas.

Before you consider this speech completely prepared, construct the outline at the end of this project.

How to Present a Bodily Action and Gesture Speech

When you make this speech, approach the speaker's stand with the attitude of a person determined to win. Have no fear that your gestures and actions will be wrong or inappropriate. Take pride in the fact that you are going to use your entire organism in speaking. With this attitude you cannot lose.

When you actually present your speech, concentrate on one point which will make the audience *understand* what you are informing them about. They have to understand you, or you will not be getting your ideas across (communicating). Now, while you are earnestly presenting your ideas, try to make them clearer by demonstrating what you have to say. Do this by acting out certain parts as you talk. If you tell the audience that it is best to mount a horse a certain way, show them how to do it. If you say a baseball should be thrown a certain way, demonstrate it with all the force and energy you would use were you actually pitching. If your demonstration is so vigorous that it makes you short of breath, so much the better; you will have been truly trying to *show*, as well as tell what you have to say. You may exhibit pictures, charts, diagrams, write on the blackboard. If you do, be sure that your equipment is ready for exhibition before you begin.

BIBLIOGRAPHY

Borchers & Wise, chap. 2.
Borden, pp. 92-101.
Brigance & Immel, chaps. 4-6.
Bryant & Wallace, *Fund.*, pp. 337-339.
Crocker, *Pub. Spkg.*, chap. 4.
Dolman, chap. 16.
Hibbitt, chaps. 7,8.

Monroe, *Prin. & Types*, chap. 2.
Murray, chaps. 11, 12.
Norvelle & Smith, chap. 13.
O'Neill, pp. 266-268.
Sarett & Foster, chaps. 5-7.
Weaver, chap. 8.
Winans, chap. 21.
Woolbert & Weaver, pp. 45-54, 305-331.

SPEECH OUTLINE, PROJECT 8

Name . . . . Date . . . . Type of speech . . . .

Specific purpose of this speech . . . .

. . . . No. of sources required . . . . .

Sentence outline: 75-125 words.   Time limit: 4-5 minutes.   Speaking notes: None.

TITLE

INTRODUCTION

BODY

CONCLUSION

INSTRUCTOR'S COMMENTS

Clarity of purpose . . . .

Gesture-action-eye contact . . . .

Language . . . .

Voice . . . .

Enthusiasm and vigor . . . .

Self-confidence . . . .

Organization . . . .

Introduction and conclusion . . . .

Grade . . . .

(List sources on back of page as indicated)

PRINTED SOURCES OF INFORMATION

Give complete information for each source.

1. Author's name . . . .
   Title of article. . . . .
   Book or magazine containing article . . . .
   . . . . Date of publication . . . .
   Chapters and/or pages containing material . . . .

2. Author's name . . . .
   Title of article. . . . .
   Book or magazine containing article . . . .
   . . . . Date of publication . . . .
   Chapters and/or pages containing material . . . .

3. Author's name . . . .
   Title of article. . . . .
   Book or magazine containing article . . . .
   . . . . Date of publication . . . .
   Chapters and/or pages containing material. . . . .

INTERVIEW SOURCES OF INFORMATION

1. Name of person interviewed. . . . . Date of interview . . . .
   His title, position, and occupation . . . .
   . . . .
   Why is he an authority on the subject? Be specific . . . .
   . . . .

2. Name of person interviewed. . . . . Date of interview . . . .
   His title, position, and occupation . . . .
   . . . .
   Why is he an authority on the subject? Be specific. . . . .
   . . . .

3. Name of person interviewed. . . . . Date of interview . . . .
   His title, position, and occupation . . . .
   . . . .
   Why is he an authority on the subject? Be specific. . . . .
   . . . .

THE SPEECH OF FEAR CONFESSION

The speech of self-explanation and fear confession is unique. It is also important because it does a great deal for the student. By carrying it through, a student sometimes achieves a mastery over himself which before he had thought impossible. He sees that practically all inexperienced speakers suffer similar fears and physical reactions, including apathy, speechlessness, short breath, dry mouth, weak knees, pain in the stomach, and nervous trembling. Because improvement is so often an immediate result of this speech experience, it is offered here with the thought that every student will gain much from it. As you will see, it is not a speech ever to be presented to a public audience.

Explanation of the Speech of Fear Confession

This speech is absolutely unrehearsed. It requires a maximum of honesty, sincerity, understanding of the other fellow, and straight-from-the-heart truth. Without complete honesty and frankness, many benefits are lost.

When your turn to speak is called or when you volunteer, merely take the floor and honestly tell your audience about all the peculiar, strange, queer feelings you have when you talk to them. If your knees are shaking, say so; go even further — show your audience, without exaggeration, how they are shaking. In other words, *tell everything*.

You may be amused at your fears as you recount them. Your audience may be amused with you, but not at you. They undoubtedly have many of the same fears. After you have made known all your fears, the class will tell you voluntarily how they think you can overcome your various nervous tensions. After these class suggestions, it will be your turn again. You are to tell honestly how you feel at that moment. You may be surprised to find yourself calm, greatly relaxed, and poised. If not, you probably did not tell the group all your fears and are still trying to hide certain feelings which you hope your audience will not recognize. If you feel "pretty good," it is likely that you have told everything and no longer are trying to hide a great number of normal nervous reactions. Throughout this experience you are to remain standing.

Suggested Topic for the Speech of Fear Confession

You need no specific topic for this speech. Just tell how you feel before speaking, when speaking, and after you finish a speech. Also tell what you think really causes your fears.

How to Prepare a Speech of Fear Confession

Think of all the many sensations and thoughts and insignificant reactions that have flashed into your mind during your past speeches. In order not to overlook anything, write out a list of these bothersome gremlins and study them carefully so that you may orally trade stories with other class members. If something funny has happened to you because of stage fright, plan to tell the group about it. You will enjoy a good joke on yourself and so will they. It will be good mental hygiene. Your best preparation is to give yourself a definite set of mind in which you make a decision to tell everything without reservation.

How to Present a Speech of Fear Confession

This should be the simplest, most undramatic, and most sincere speech you have made. It should come straight from the heart from start to finish — nothing more, nothing less. Your style should be *you* talking with a group of friends who will reciprocate. You do not need any notes except perhaps for a simple list of the fears and sensations you want to talk about.

The order of your speech should follow these three steps:
1. Describe all your fears and sensations.
2. Ask your audience to tell you informally how they think you can improve yourself.
3. After they conclude their remarks, tell them exactly how you feel at the moment; then retire to your chair.

BIBLIOGRAPHY

Borchers & Wise, chap. 9.
Brigance, *Speech Comm.*, pp. 16-19.
Bryant & Wallace, *Fund.*, pp. 60-69.
Buehler, pp. 31-40.
Butler, chap. 1.

Crocker, *Pub. Spkg.*, chap. 2.
Eisenson, chap. 18.
Hollingsworth, chap. 13.
Murray, chap. 7.
Sarett & Foster, chap. 3.
Thompson, pp. 36-38.

PROJECT 10

THE ANNOUNCEMENT

Each year many millions of announcements are made. Each year many people who hear these announcements are left in a confused state of mind because the information presented was poorly organized, obscure, incomplete, or could not be heard. Often, as a result, attendance at clubs, schools, churches, and other organizations has been disappointing. It is true that you cannot force people to attend a gathering, but it is just as true that you can increase attendance by making absolutely certain that everyone within hearing distance of your voice is fully informed about the event you are announcing.

Explanation of an Announcement

An announcement is a presentation of information. It is brief, concise, to the point, and pertinent. It tells specifically about something in the past (who won a prize), about events to occur immediately (the governor will appear in one minute, or there will be an important business meeting following adjournment); it may concern a dance to be sponsored next month. An announcement should be crystal-clear in meaning, contain all necessary and helpful data, be stated in easily understandable terms, and be heard by everyone present. Occasions for its use arise at practically every kind of meeting. Recently radio and television have offered a convenient medium for making announcements.

Suggested Announcements

Choose two or three of the following suggestions as bases for announcements:

1. A college election.
2. A labor meeting.
3. A skating party tomorrow night.
4. A picnic next week.
5. An all-school play next week.
6. A football game.
7. A basketball game.
8. A convention.
9. A special Christmas sale.
10. A new bus schedule.
11. A lecture.
12. A new schedule for classes.
13. A hunting expedition.
14. A ski meet.
15. The showing of a new car.
16. The demonstration of a new machine.
17. New closing hours for the library.
18. A wrestling match.
19. A golf tournament.
20. Speaker's choice.

How to Choose an Announcement

Study the above suggestions closely. Check the ones that attract you. From these select two or three that you think you would enjoy, as well as profit from announcing. Make up your mind now, so that you will have ample time to prepare the information for your announcements.

How to Prepare an Announcement

The chief purpose of an announcement is to inform. Keep this in mind as you prepare your material. Organize your information as you would organize any good speech. Have an interesting introduction and a strong conclusion, as well as good organization of the other necessary material.

Your first job will be to gather information. Be sure to secure this from authentic and authoritative sources. Do not rely on hearsay. Be absolutely certain that your data are accurate and correct to the last detail. If there is any doubt at all, recheck the material before presenting your announcement. It is your responsibility to have all the last-minute information available. Ascertain whether any changes have occurred since you first received your information.

The organization of your announcement is important. Present your information in logical sequence. Give the most important part first. The rest of your announcement should follow in the order of importance.

Generally, the order of presenting items may be similar to the following. Show that the event is timely and opportune. If there are known or probable objections, refute them impersonally; however, avoid going into defensive debate or offering a long list of excuses for the action your announcement proposes. Name the exact place of the meeting and its location. Tell how to get there, if this is necessary, and indicate the advantage of the place. Give the date, the day, and the exact hour. If there is an admission charge, state the price or prices. If desirable, tell about the reasonableness of the charges and where the money will go, especially when the project is a worthy one. If there are tickets, tell where, when, and how they may be secured. If reserved seats are available, explain any special conditions concerning them. Finally, summarize by restating the occasion, the place, the time, and the admission. (Not all of the above points have to be included in every announcement. Your own judgment will tell you what should be omitted or added, as the case may be.) Do not say "I thank you" when you finish.

Prepare notes to be used in making your announcements so that nothing essential will be omitted. Use cards at least three by five inches in size. Make your notes brief, orderly, and legible. Rehearse them until you have everything well in mind.

How to Present an Announcement

Your attitude will be one of alertness and politeness. There will be no great need for bodily action other than that which naturally accompanies what you have to say. Speak clearly and distinctly. All places, dates, days, and times must be articulated so that there can be no misunderstanding.

Your place should be before the audience where all can see and hear you, not back in an obscure corner or elsewhere among the crowd. Go to the front and stand near the center of the platform. Observe good posture. Pause until you have gained the attention of the audience. Your first words should be heard by everyone. In some cases you may need to raise your hand or rap on a table to get attention. However, do not attempt to talk above crowd noises if the audience is slow to respond. When referring to your notes, hold them up so that you can see them and still keep your eyes on the audience; avoid talking to the floor. When you finish, go back to your seat unostentatiously. There should be no display in your entire performance. Pleasantness and the desire to be understood are enough.

BIBLIOGRAPHY

Baker, chap. 6.   Buehler, part 2, chap. 6.   Butler, chap. 4.

SPEECH OUTLINE, PROJECT 10

Name .... Date ....

Prepare two or more announcements with a 20- to 40-word complete sentence outline for each. Time limit: 2-4 minutes (total for all announcements combined).

What is your specific purpose?...
....

First Announcement
Introduction:

Body:

Conclusion:

Second Announcement
Introduction:

Body:

Conclusion:

Third Announcement
Introduction:

Body:

Conclusion:

INSTRUCTOR'S COMMENTS

Clarity of purpose . . . .

Gesture-action-eye contact . . . .

Language . . . .

Voice . . . .

Enthusiasm and vigor . . . .

Self-confidence . . . .

Organization . . . .

Introduction and conclusion . . . .

Grade . . . .

(List sources on back of page as indicated)

(34)

PROJECT 11

INTRODUCING A SPEAKER

Many untrained speakers are asked to give introduction speeches. Some introductions are well done, but far too many are haphazard and embarrassing because the persons making them are untrained. This brings criticism upon the person who must present a speaker and it also weakens programs that feature lecturers. Of all the types of speeches you may make in the future, it is probable that one of them will be the introduction of a featured speaker.

Explanation of the Introduction Speech

An introduction speech is one in which a chairman or other person introduces a speaker to an audience. The purpose is to bring an audience and speaker together in the proper spirit. Several of the requirements follow. The speech should be short; it should make the audience and speaker feel comfortably acquainted; it should interest the audience in the speaker and his subject; it should put the speaker at ease, give his name, and announce his subject.

The introducer should avoid attempts at being funny. He should never embarrass the speaker either by heaping too much praise upon him or by belittling him. The person introducing a speaker should not call attention to himself or say or do anything to detract from what the speaker plans to say. The person who said, "Get up, speak up, shut up," probably was thinking of the individual who makes introduction speeches; and the introducer can hardly go wrong if he follows this advice. However, on certain occasions when humor is expected, toastmasters utilize unique introductions as a means of attaining humor.

Occasions for the introduction speech arise every time a speaker is introduced. They probably number in the millions annually.

Suggested Introduction Speeches
1. Introduce a minister to a college audience.
2. Introduce the college dean to the freshman class.
3. Introduce a lecturer to the student body.
4. Introduce an actor to your class.
5. Introduce the college president to a public gathering.
6. A famous scientist visits your school. Introduce him.
7. Introduce a missionary at a religious meeting.
8. A navy hero speaks. Introduce him.
9. A noted industrialist speaks. Introduce him.
10. A great author speaks. Introduce him.
11. A famous musician will lecture. Introduce him.
12. The senator visits your city and school. Introduce him.
13. A high government official is the speaker. Introduce him.
14. Introduce a commencement speaker.
15. Introduce a baccalaureate speaker.
16. Introduce a manufacturer to an audience.
17. Introduce a bank president to a civic organization.
18. Introduce a Hollywood celebrity to your school.
19. Introduce the city fire marshal.
20. Speaker's choice.

How to Choose an Introduction Speech

Look over the list of suggestions above. If you like one of them, select it. If not, you may have some other topic which you prefer. If this is the case, make up your mind without delay and start thinking about your speech. You will have to decide for yourself as to the type of imaginary audience and occasion you will use. You will also find it necessary to decide concerning the specific person you plan to introduce. Be sure that your speaker is a suitable one for the occasion. Above all, do not attempt to be different by improvising a speech built around a classmate whom you place in an impossible or ludicrous position. This will defeat you as a speaker and will not meet the assignment.

How to Prepare an Introduction Speech

In preparing this speech you may draw your information from four sources: the speaker, his subject, the audience, or the occasion. Not all of these may be necessary in every speech; often, however, they are all suitable. You will not need much material, but what you have must be accurate and pertinent. As for the speaker, get his name and be absolutely certain you have it right. Know how to pronounce it correctly. Discover any of his background that should be known by the audience. This may concern his education, special training, travel experience, special honors, membership in organizations, important positions he has held, books he has written, or any other notable achievements. Of course, if he is a famous and well-known person, little need be said, possibly nothing. An example of the latter is the often-heard introduction:"Ladies and gentlemen, the President." However, almost all speakers require more introduction than does the President of the United States, or a governor or other high state official. You should know the title of the speaker's subject. As with his name, *have it right*, but say nothing about the speech that will tend to "steal its thunder." Inquire thoroughly into the make-up of your audience so that you may adjust your remarks to them. The occasion for the address should be well known to you. From the four sources just mentioned and a fifth — yourself — construct your introduction speech. Short though this speech is to be, what you say must really count. Thus, you must organize and arrange it carefully, selecting those bits of information that are most important.

Before your ideas "set," you should confer, at least in imagination, with the person you are going to introduce and arrive at a definite understanding regarding what you plan to say in your introduction speech. After this is decided, rehearse aloud until you are confident that you are thoroughly prepared.

How to Present an Introduction Speech

When the moment arrives for you to introduce the speaker of the evening, rise calmly, take your place on the platform, pause until the room grows quiet, and then deliberately address the audience in your normal voice. Speak loudly enough for all to hear, but avoid straining or using greater force than is needed. You may say, "Ladies and gentlemen," or use some other expression appropriate to the audience and the occasion.

Your bodily actions and gestures will be limited; there will probably be no necessity for using either more than moderately. Your voice should be well modulated, the words spoken clearly, and your pronunciation correct — especially when you say the speaker's name.

Keep in mind your part of the occasion. People did not come to hear you or see you. You are only a convenient but necessary cog in the chain of events surrounding the speaker. Your poise and confidence and appropriate but brief remarks are all that are expected or wanted from you. You may greet the audience and mention the occasion, extend felicitations, and note that there is an exceptionally good audience (if there is). If there is a poor audience, do not remark about it and do not make any apologies.

At the moment you present the speaker, announce his name and subject somewhat as follows: "I am happy to present Mr. A., who will address you (or speak to you) on . . . . (mention the subject)." Then turn to the speaker with the words, "Mr. A." You may bow slightly or nod and take your seat when he rises and comes to the front of the platform.

If you are chairman of the assembly, it is appropriate for you to express the audience's appreciation publicly to the speaker at the conclusion of his address.

BIBLIOGRAPHY

Borden, pp. 35-39.
Brigance, *Speech Comp.*, pp. 300-303.
Bryant & Wallace, *Fund.*, pp. 546-550.
Buehler, part 2, chap. 6.

Carnegie, pp. 455-457.
Crocker, *Pub. Spkg.*, chap. 22.
Glasgow, pp. 161-164.
Hibbitt, pp. 203-204.

Name . . . . Date . . . . Type of speech . . . .

Specific purpose of this speech . . . . ▪

. . . . No. of sources required . . . .

Sentence outline: 50-100 words.   Time limit: 1-2 minutes.   Speaking notes: None.

TITLE

INTRODUCTION

BODY

CONCLUSION

INSTRUCTOR'S COMMENTS

   Clarity of purpose . . . .

   Gesture-action-eye contact . . . .

   Language . . . .

   Voice . . . .

   Enthusiasm and vigor . . . .

   Self-confidence . . . .

   Organization . . . .

   Introduction and conclusion . . . .

   Grade . . . .

(List sources on back of page as indicated)

PRINTED SOURCES OF INFORMATION

Give complete information for each source.

1. Author's name . . . .
   Title of article. . . . .
   Book or magazine containing article . . . .
   . . . . Date of publication . . . .
   Chapters and/or pages containing material . . . .
2. Author's name . . . .
   Title of article. . . . .
   Book or magazine containing article . . . .
   . . . . Date of publication . . . .
   Chapters and/or pages containing material . . . .
3. Author's name . . . .
   Title of article. . . . .
   Book or magazine containing article . . . .
   . . . . Date of publication . . . .
   Chapters and/or pages containing material . . . .

INTERVIEW SOURCES OF INFORMATION

1. Name of person interviewed . . . . Date of interview . . . .
   His title, position, and occupation . . . .
   . . . .
   Why is he an authority on the subject? Be specific . . . .
   . . . .
2. Name of person interviewed . . . . Date of interview . . . .
   His title, position, and occupation . . . .
   . . . .
   Why is he an authority on the subject? Be specific . . . .
   . . . .
3. Name of person interviewed . . . . Date of interview . . . .
   His title, position, and occupation . . . .
   . . . .
   Why is he an authority on the subject? Be specific . . . .
   . . . .

PROJECT 12

THE SPEECH TO INFORM – ANY SUBJECT

No one knows how many speeches are given each year. Neither does anyone know exactly what kinds of speeches are presented. We do know, however, that of the millions and millions of talks, many are made specifically to inform people – to tell them something they will find beneficial to include in their knowledge. While no one can foretell accurately what kind of speeches you will be called upon to present in the future, it is a safe bet that many times you will speak to inform people. Because so many speeches are informative in nature, you are offered here the opportunity to become acquainted with this type of speech.

Explanation of the Speech to Inform

The informative speech provides an audience with a clear understanding of the speaker's ideas on a subject. It also arouses interest. This means that the audience must understand and comprehend fully what the speaker is talking about. Their grasp of his subject should be as fundamental as he can possibly make it in the time allotted him. The information he presents should not be offered in such a way that he seems to be attempting to convince people about a certain point of view. Humor is highly desirable in an informative speech. Usually there is not enough of it; however, it should not be used to excess so that the speech becomes one to entertain. When the speaker concludes, his audience should feel that they have really been given a wealth of material on a subject which they previously had not understood at all well. If you can make them say when they are leaving, "Now I understand that problem; it was certainly cleared up in my mind tonight," you can be satisfied that your speech was informative – just as you intended it to be.

To accomplish the ends of informative speaking, the speaker is obliged to select a subject of interest to himself and his listeners. This can be done by an apt analysis of the audience – in this case your classmates. You as the speaker are charged further with the serious responsibility of knowing what you are talking about – knowing more about it, in fact, than anyone in your audience does. For this reason, your talk demands that you study several sources of information. Under no consideration should you be satisfied to glance hurriedly through an article in a popular magazine, jot down a few notes, and toss the periodical aside. This kind of work does not even begin to prepare you to give an informative discourse.

Occasions for the informative speech are many. They arise on the lecture platform, in the pulpit, in the classroom, at business meetings – in fact, wherever you find reports being made, instructions given, or ideas being presented by means of lectures and discussions. The point to bear in mind is that whenever information is disseminated, an occasion for an informative speech arises.

Suggested Topics for Speeches to Inform

1. Marriage customs in Japan.
2. Peculiar customs of China.
3. Jet propulsion—explain by diagram.
4. Hunting techniques in Africa.
5. Sports (how to play a certain game).
6. How to dance the rhumba.
7. Boat racing—give rules.
8. Swimming techniques—demonstrate.
9. The story of gold.
10. The life of a great man.
11. The land of the Eskimo.
12. How to predict the weather.
13. New inventions that save work.
14. Precious stones and their value.
15. History of your city.
16. Proper social etiquette.
17. New styles in houses.
18. The U.S. mints.
19. Great magicians.
20. Speaker's choice.

How to Choose a Topic

Study the above list carefully. Select something that interests you and is appropriate to the audience you are to address. Be sure that you can find information about the topic you select.

How to Prepare a Speech to Inform

To prepare for this speech, or any speech, you must know and follow certain fundamentals of preparation. These consist of the following steps: (1) Analyze the occasion; (2) choose your subject; (3) diagnose the audience; (4) gather your material; (5) organize and support your main points with evidence; (6) word your speech by writing it out in full or in part, or by rehearsing it from an outline; (7) practice aloud.

If you wish to organize your thoughts logically, decide early what objective you hope to attain and what reaction you want from this particular audience. Next, if you wish, you may divide your discourse into three conventional parts: introduction, body, and conclusion. To be more effective, some speakers break down their talks by using various combinations of the following steps: (1) Gain attention; (2) make the audience want to hear their ideas; (3) present ideas; (4) tell why this material is important to the listeners and how it affects them; (5) ask the audience to study the topic further or to take some action on it. The time required for any one division of a speech varies greatly; however, more time is given to the presentation of ideas than to any other part.

The wording of your talk may be accomplished either by writing it out in full from the outline, or by doing considerable practice. In any event, rehearse before a mirror as many times as necessary to fix the proper steps in your mind and the order of their content, along with desirable stage appearance and bodily action. Do not memorize the words.

The use of notes is somewhat a matter of opinion. If you are adequately prepared, you will not need them for you will talk extemporaneously; this is the most effective method known. If you must refer to notes, they should be short sentences, phrases, or single words which have a particular meaning to you. Whatever the notes you use, they should be brief, concise, meaningful, and entirely familiar. A glance at them should be sufficient to give you their full meaning so that you can speak fluently yet logically.

One other point is important. The information you present must be accurate. For accuracy of information, acceptable sources and reliable and competent authorities must be consulted. Your audience should know where you get your material. You are the person to identify these sources and authorities. You are expected to go even further in this matter of giving information, for you are expected to offer your own conclusions and views and evaluations of your information. All this entails your neat assimilation of all you have pulled together, that is, your entire speech.

A few hints might well be offered at this point. First, have only two or three main points to your speech. Buttress these well with examples, illustrations, analogies, and facts. Second, do not be afraid to inject humor and anecdotes into your thought to add interest. Be sure these additions are suited to your subject and audience. Third, be sure your speech moves ahead. Do not allow it to drag. Last, exert plenty of effort toward having an interesting introduction and an equally effective conclusion.

Outline Your Speech

Outlining your speech is necessary if you wish to secure organization, a logical order of material, coherence, and unity. Without these rhetorical qualities, your thoughts will be a jumbled mass of words with little direction and no definite goal.

After you have constructed your 75-150-word sentence outline, be prepared to hand it to your instructor when you rise to speak. He will undoubtedly wish to follow it while listening to your speech. State two or three sources of information. Read at least two references on outlining.

How to Present a Speech to Inform

Use an easy, energetic presentation. Be enthusiastic and original in what you have to say. Use your hands to demonstrate how to do things. Draw pictures, show charts — in fact, do whatever is necessary to make your ideas understood and interesting. Take the stage properly, utilize expressive bodily action, maintain direct eye contact, observe time limits, and stop when your speech is finished. Your conclusion should be as strong and appropriate and as well prepared as your beginning remarks.

BIBLIOGRAPHY

Borchers & Wise, chaps. 8, 13.
Brigance, *Speech Comm.*, chap. 4.
Brigance, *Speech Comp.*, chap. 3.
Buehler, part 2, chap. 4.

Gray & Braden, chap. 8.
Monroe, *Prin. & Types*, chap. 16.
Norvelle & Smith, chap. 3.
Thompson, part 2.

Name . . . . Date . . . . Type of speech . . . .

Specific purpose of this speech . . . .

. . . . No. of sources required . . . . . .

Sentence outline: 75-150 words.   Time limit: 4-5 minutes.   Speaking notes: None.

TITLE

INTRODUCTION

BODY

CONCLUSION

INSTRUCTOR'S COMMENTS

Clarity of purpose . . . .

Gesture-action-eye contact . . . .

Language . . . .

Voice . . . .

Enthusiasm and vigor . . . .

Self-confidence . . . .

Organization . . . .

Introduction and conclusion . . . .

Grade . . . .

(List sources on back of page as indicated)

PRINTED SOURCES OF INFORMATION

Give complete information for each source.

1. Author's name ....
   Title of article ....
   Book or magazine containing article ....
   .... Date of publication ....
   Chapters and/or pages containing material ....

2. Author's name ....
   Title of article ....
   Book or magazine containing article ....
   .... Date of publication ....
   Chapters and/or pages containing material ....

3. Author's name ....
   Title of article ....
   Book or magazine containing article ....
   .... Date of publication ....
   Chapters and/or pages containing material ....

INTERVIEW SOURCES OF INFORMATION

1. Name of person interviewed .... Date of interview ....
   His title, position, and occupation ....
   ....
   Why is he an authority on the subject? Be specific ....
   ....

2. Name of person interviewed .... Date of interview ....
   His title, position, and occupation ....
   ....
   Why is he an authority on the subject? Be specific ....
   ....

3. Name of person interviewed .... Date of interview ....
   His title, position, and occupation ....
   ....
   Why is he an authority on the subject? Be specific ....
   ....

PROJECT 13

THE GOOD-WILL SPEECH

One type of speech utilized many thousands of times each year is the kind that secures good will from an audience. The popularity and usefulness of good-will speeches are not likely to decline, but rather to grow. Your place in society may at any time demand that you join the parade of those who make speeches designed to secure good will. Because this type of speech occurs so often, you should, by all means, have experience with it.

Explanation of the Good-Will Speech

A speech to gain good will is one whose purpose is to secure a favorable attitude toward the speaker and the group he represents. Normally, this speech is made to a friendly audience, which necessitates the presentation of what might easily be called a speech to inform. This is the apparent purpose, as far as the audience is concerned. However, the thought behind the presentation of information is this: by causing his listeners to understand and appreciate the group he represents, the speaker will secure their good will.

Occasions for good-will speeches arise at luncheons, club meetings, special demonstrations, school meetings, religious gatherings, conventions, business meetings. Any group that convenes to hear a speaker give them information, whether it be a straight informative talk, an illustrated lecture, the showing of a film, or the demonstration of a new product, is likely to be the recipient of a good-will speech. We might classify a good-will speech as a subtle or indirect sales talk.

Suggested Topics and Audiences

Construct a good-will speech in which you represent a certain group on a definite occasion.
1. Represent an oil company to a civic club.
2. Represent a chemical manufacturing corporation to a Chamber of Commerce.
3. Represent a soap manufacturing company to a Lions Club.
4. Tell how your company makes ladies' hose — to a sorority.
5. Represent a perfume company to a group of women.
6. Represent a book company to a group of students.
7. Represent a college to a high school.
8. Represent a toy company to a group of young mothers.
9. Represent a speech school to a woman's club.
10. Represent the senior class to the freshman class.
11. Represent your fraternity to another fraternity.
12. Represent a tourist agency at a teachers' meeting.
13. Represent an implement company at a Farm Bureau meeting.
14. Represent a night school to a group of businessmen.
15. Represent the R.O.T.C. to a student body.
16. Represent a city in another city.
17. Represent a newspaper before a civic group.
18. Represent a political party at a college assembly.
19. Represent a drug store before a group of businessmen.
20. Speaker's choice.

How to Choose a Topic

As always, choose a topic that has a compelling interest for you. Choose one you know something about; one about which you can get more information. Make your selection without delay.

How to Prepare a Good-Will Speech

First of all, remember that your purpose is to secure good will. Second, do not forget that your remarks will be necessarily of an informative nature. We will assume that you have analyzed your audience and selected your topic.

(43)

As soon as you have done this, begin to gather your materials. Practically all large companies and corporations will gladly send you information if you write for it. Many local business houses and Chambers of Commerce will provide pamphlets and brochures. Encyclopedias and Readers' Guides are excellent sources. If you are willing to use a reasonable amount of initiative, you will have no difficulty in locating materials to supplement your own knowledge. If you reach an impasse, ask your instructor for assistance.

After you have gathered your material, organize it logically so that it can be easily followed. Decide on the order, the arrangement, the illustrations and examples, an effective introduction, and a strong conclusion. In other words, the entire pattern of your speech must be worked out carefully.

There are several characteristics of the good-will speech to note. Be sure you have interesting facts, new material —novel or out-of-the-ordinary subject matter that your listeners have not heard before. Show a definite relationship between your corporation, institution, profession, and the lives of your listeners. They should be made to see that their happiness and prosperity are tied in with your activities or those which you represent. In making this point do not ask their approval or request their approbation; take it for granted that they already approve. And last, if possible offer them a definite service, in the form of souvenirs, samples, or an invitation to visit your plant, city, or institution. It could be in the form of special favors or accommodations to members of the audience, or merely the answering of questions they care to raise at the conclusion of your remarks. Above all, be willing to help your audience — you are at their service. (Do not forget to practice this speech aloud before you present it to your audience.)

How to Present a Good-Will Speech

This is a speech in which friendliness, good humor, and modesty count to a high degree. You will be talking about yourself and your organization. Bragging has no place. The information you present will have to be strong and interesting enough to do its own talking. Be tolerant of your competitors and gracious in your appraisal of them. Be careful about forcing your material on your audience. If you possess the necessary good feeling and friendliness for your auditors, they will reciprocate these attitudes.

Give attention to your posture; be alert and eager to communicate. Talk to be heard and understood. Avoid unnecessary formality. Bodily action and gesture are in order, as always, if they are used appropriately. Avoid being suave and bland; just be friendly and sincere.

BIBLIOGRAPHY

Butler, chaps. 1-4.   Monroe, *Prin. & Types*, chap. 22.   Monroe, *Prin.* pp. 229-245.

Name . . . . Date . . . . Type of speech . . . .

Specific purpose of this speech . . . .

. . . . No. of sources required . . . . . .

Sentence outline: 75-150 words.   Time limit: 6-7 minutes.   Speaking notes: None.

TITLE

INTRODUCTION

BODY

CONCLUSION

INSTRUCTOR'S COMMENTS

   Clarity of purpose. . . . .

   Gesture-action-eye contact . . . .

   Language . . . .

   Voice. . . . .

   Enthusiasm and vigor . . . .

   Self-confidence . . . .

   Organization . . . .

   Introduction and conclusion . . . .

   Grade . . . .

(List sources on back of page as indicated)

PRINTED SOURCES OF INFORMATION

Give complete information for each source.

1. Author's name ....
   Title of article..
   Book or magazine containing article ....
   .... Date of publication...............
   Chapters and/or pages containing material ....
2. Author's name ....
   Title of article..
   Book or magazine containing article ....
   .... Date of publication...............
   Chapters and/or pages containing material ....
3. Author's name ....
   Title of article..
   Book or magazine containing article ....
   .... Date of publication...............
   Chapters and/or pages containing material ....

INTERVIEW SOURCES OF INFORMATION

1. Name of person interviewed....................... Date of interview.........
   His title, position, and occupation ....
   ....
   Why is he an authority on the subject? Be specific...............................
   ....
2. Name of person interviewed....................... Date of interview..........
   His title, position, and occupation ....
   ....
   Why is he an authority on the subject? Be specific...............................
   ....
3. Name of person interviewed....................... Date of interview..........
   His title, position, and occupation ....
   ....
   Why is he an authority on the subject? Be specific...............................
   ....

PROJECT 14

THE SPECIAL REPORT

"As the significance and complexity of projects increase, the time available to a speaker to explain thoroughly these projects to appropriate groups often decreases. A speaker may have ten minutes to explain a simple project but may be allowed only twenty minutes to explain a project a hundred times as complex. It is therefore important that a speaker be able to analyze data and reduce them to their significant elements, avoiding both meaningless generalities and confusing detail. Perhaps nowhere is the need to be precise greater than in the special report."

The above statement was made by a well-known educator who through experience has learned the importance of the special report. Students will do well to follow his advice in learning how to prepare and present a special report.

Explanation of the Special Report

The special report is an informative speech prepared because someone or a group of individuals needs certain definite and specific information. It generally requires an investigation of literature or of on-the-spot conditions involving original research. It may require a combination of these two methods of securing information. Its purpose is to provide a clear understanding of all the data, factual information, and recommendations which are contained in it.

The special report may concern the financial condition of a business, information on engineering, personnel, labor conditions, salaries, wages, marketing, distribution, or many other aspects of business, or conditions relating to any kind of enterprise or situation. It may pertain to past events or to present conditions, or it may be an investigation made solely for the purpose of providing information on which to base future action.

In a special report no effort is made to persuade or to influence action or belief. Recommendations may be made at the conclusion of the report if wanted or needed; they generally provide the basis for future action or change of belief.

Incomplete special reports may be presented at various stages of their development. There are two kinds. The first is a *preliminary report* which is limited to incomplete data covering only as far as the investigation has gone. It may outline plans for further investigation. The second is a *report of the progress* made thus far in the investigation. It generally presents more extensive information, tentative conclusions, and further plans relative to the investigation.

Occasions for special reports arise any time special information is needed. Such reports are made to business managements, and to governing bodies of any organization, be it civic, religious, educational, financial, agricultural, governmental, political, or otherwise.

Suggested Topics for the Special Report

1. Report on attendance at local football games for the past five seasons. Is a new stadium needed?
2. Report on library conditions to determine whether or not a new library is needed.
3. Is present athletic equipment adequate? Report.
4. Should a traffic light be placed at a certain intersection? Report.
5. How much money is needed to operate the school during the coming year? Report.
6. Should the teaching staff of your college be increased? Report.
7. Should more parking space be provided for student and faculty cars? Report.
8. Would it be advisable to install a college cafeteria? Report.
9. Should Blank fraternity build a fraternity house? Report.
10. Should the city's main street be widened? Report.
11. What is the present condition of the fire department? Report.
12. Would it be advisable to provide more water for the city? Report.
13. Are city traffic regulations adequate? Report.
14. Should more money be provided for publication of the school paper? Report.
15. Should the city purchase land for a new park? Report.

16. Is the number of tardy students large enough so that they should be penalized for tardiness? Report.
17. Should a new school health program be established? Report.
18. Should dormitory hours be changed? Report.
19. Is more student housing needed? Report.
20. Speaker's choice.

How to Choose a Topic

In choosing a topic to investigate for a special report, make sure you select one about which you can find complete information. Remember that in some instances you will have to do considerable research and checking of records besides original on-the-spot investigation. Keep in mind when selecting your topic that you are not going to try to prove anything one way or another but that you are going to investigate all the angles of your topic and then report impartially what you find out. Since much work may be required to gather your information you will be wise to select a topic at once so that you will have time to conduct a thorough investigation.

How to Prepare a Special Report

In preparing a special report, bear in mind that your purpose is to present data, other information, conclusions (tentative or final), interpretations, and recommendations so that your listeners will have a clear understanding of all your information. You are not to attempt to persuade them or to get action from them. You simply lay the results of your findings before your audience in the most understandable way you can.

Another point is this. Most special reporting is done because someone, a group of persons, or a business needs to secure certain specific information so that they may proceed with new action, continue their present action, or cease an action. What the reporter discovers may form the basis of their future action. Hence it is of the utmost importance that the report be complete and accurate.

A reliable method for preparing a report follows:

Learn specifically what you are supposed to investigate and what your report will be used for. You can see at a glance that you will have to do two things. First, find out what information is needed, and second, go after the information before drawing up your report. An example might be: "Should the Blank Oil Company buy a certain property and construct a service station on it?" Here it would be necessary to investigate all the costs of acquiring the property and to become familiar with building restrictions, fire protection, tax rates, adjoining businesses, competitive neighborhood stations, number of motor vehicles passing the location daily, etc. After getting this information you would prepare your report.

Another example might be as follows: Suppose a factory needed to learn the number of man-hours lost because of sickness and injuries among employees over a three-month period. Their problem is whether or not they should set up, equip, and staff more first-aid stations in the factory. You can easily visualize the task of investigation. Here you will not try to count sick people as they leave the factory but you will go to the company books and dig out the needed information for a previous three-month period. In this case you will examine records. This is comparable to investigating any literature to secure needed information. You will prepare your report after your information is collected.

You can gather investigatory data by correspondence, reading, personal interviews, field investigation, and laboratory research. A combination of all these methods is often required.

Organizing the Special Report

We now consider the organization of your report. Since the organization of most special reports is similar, the following plan is recommended:

INTRODUCTION
1. Prepare your introduction. (This may be done last.)
2. State the reasons for your report. (A brief history may be included.)

3. State the purpose of your report and the problem you were investigating. Be specific.
    A. State any limitations and particular objectives or points which were considered.
4. Name your sources of data. *Be specific for all sources.*
5. Explain clearly your method of securing data. Tell about special records which you examined, identify persons you interviewed, and state where and when. Describe any special tools, equipment, instruments, or other mechanical devices you used in getting data. State places, times, dates, and anything else relevant to describing your method of securing information.
6. State generally what the main ideas in your report will concern.

BODY
  I. Present your first main finding.
    A. Give a subfinding — if there is one — to substantiate your first main finding.
      1. Present data to verify your subfinding.
    B. Give another subfinding — if there is one — to substantiate your first main finding.
      1. Present data to verify this subfinding.
 II. Present your second main finding.
    A. Give a subfinding — if there is one — to substantiate your second main finding.
      1. Present data to verify your subfinding.
    B. Give another subfinding — if there is one — to substantiate your second main finding.
      1. Present data to verify this subfinding.
Present as many more main findings and subfindings as necessary.

CONCLUSION
  I. Summarize your findings.
 II. Summarize the significance of your findings.
III. When requested, make recommendations regarding the problem you were investigating. You may recommend that further investigation should be made or that certain action should or should not be taken, or you may combine the two. (Do not strive to have your recommendations adopted. Other persons will decide this on the basis of your complete report.)

In organizing your material, select only the main findings or your summaries of them, and list them in the order of significance and importance. Often the people who listen to a report are interested only in the main ideas it contains. Hence an oral report does not contain much detail. Too much detail will probably be more confusing than clarifying because people simply cannot grasp everything that is presented. A written version of the oral report, including all details, should be prepared for study at a later date.

How to Present a Special Report
In the special report, as in any speech, you should observe all the elements that contribute to effective speaking. Everything should be well prepared and well rehearsed. Your language should be clear and vivid. It is probable that you will make your report to a group of specialists who will understand the terminolgy and technical terms you may use. However, if the audience is composed of laymen you must use understandable nontechnical language. It is also probable that interest in your report will be more than average because persons who are concerned about the special information you have will make up your audience. This should not be interpreted to mean that your report should be dry and dull. Rather your efforts should be directed toward using language that is descriptive, concrete, and concise so that complete understanding can be gained. Make your report as interesting as possible.

If diagrams, charts, graphs, or other illustrations are used they should be ready for instant use during your report. You should be entirely familiar with them. They should be placed so that everyone can see them easily and they should be large enough to be easily read.

Talk audibly and clearly. Your voice should be distinct, well articulated, and loud enough for all to hear easily. Speak at a speed which can readily be followed and comprehended; 125 to 160 words per minute is probably about right. Naturally you should sound both confident and pleasant.

After your report is concluded, be prepared to answer questions from your audience if the occasion permits. It is also desirable to have written copies of your report available for those who want them.

There are several kinds of reports besides the special report which we have just discussed. Some of the more common are the following:

1. In the *sales report*, a person reports on the sales he has made. He includes all information relative to the sale — data regarding the time of day when the sale was made, place, office conditions, general environment, method used in making the sale, statistical information, and any special features or unique aspects of the sale. The reporter is impersonal and objective in relating this information. This type of report concerns a limited group and is unique because it deals only with sales.

2. In the *committee report,* the chairman reports for his committee. He acts as spokesman for his group. All essential findings and recommendations which the committee adopted are included. Before the chairman makes the final report it is sometimes wise to have the committee approve the report to make sure that all necessary information is included. The report should present important details and deliberations that contribute to a clearer understanding of the committee's actions. Each item should be lucid and to the point. Often it is a good plan to number or letter the individual items. Recommendations should be held to a minimum; six or seven are generally sufficient. The entire report should be logically arranged.

   Frequently the committee delegates full authority to the chairman to present the report without their final approval. In this case strict impartiality on the part of the chairman should be carefully observed. A written copy of the report is usually desirable so that a permanent record of the committee findings will be on file.

3. The *personal experience report* gives the time, place, and description of the situation and environment in which personal experiences occurred. All such events should be accurately and objectively reported in the proper sequence. The individual making this report should recount these events as he experienced them. He should also show their significance to each other, and any relationship that exists among them. An example of a personal experience report is a police officer's report to his superior officer about the capture of a criminal.

BIBLIOGRAPHY

Baird & Knower, pp. 337-342.

Hibbitt, pp. 213-214.

Huston & Sandberg, pp. 99-105.

Monroe, *Prin. & Types*, pp. 19-21, 387-388.

Rogers, chap. 17.

Sandford & Yeager, *Prac. Bus. Spkg.*, chap. 9.

Sandford & Yeager, *Prin.*, pp. 315-323.

SPEECH OUTLINE, PROJECT 14

Name . . . . Date . . . . Type of speech . . . .

Specific purpose of this speech . . . .

. . . . No. of sources required . . . . . .

Sentence outline: 75-150 words.   Time: 4-5 minutes unless otherwise assigned.

Speaking notes: Brief and few unless factual data require more.

TITLE

INTRODUCTION

BODY

CONCLUSION

INSTRUCTOR'S COMMENTS

Clarity of purpose . . . .

Gesture-action-eye contact . . . .

Language . . . .

Voice . . . .

Enthusiasm and vigor . . . .

Self-confidence . . . .

Organization . . . .

Introduction and conclusion . . . .

Grade . . . .

(List sources on back of page as indicated)

PRINTED SOURCES OF INFORMATION

Give complete information for each source.

1. Author's name . . . .
   Title of article . . . .
   Book or magazine containing article . . . .
   . . . . Date of publication . . . .
   Chapters and/or pages containing material . . . .
2. Author's name . . . .
   Title of article . . . .
   Book or magazine containing article . . . .
   . . . . Date of publication . . . .
   Chapters and/or pages containing material . . . .
3. Author's name . . . .
   Title of article . . . .
   Book or magazine containing article . . . .
   . . . . Date of publication . . . .
   Chapters and/or pages containing material . . . .

INTERVIEW SOURCES OF INFORMATION

1. Name of person interviewed . . . . Date of interview . . . .
   His title, position, and occupation . . . .
   . . . .
   Why is he an authority on the subject? Be specific . . . .
   . . . .
2. Name of person interviewed . . . . Date of interview . . . .
   His title, position, and occupation . . . .
   . . . .
   Why is he an authority on the subject? Be specific . . . .
   . . . .
3. Name of person interviewed . . . . Date of interview . . . .
   His title, position, and occupation . . . .
   . . . .
   Why is he an authority on the subject? Be specific . . . .
   . . . .

THE SPEECH TO CONVINCE – ANY SUBJECT

A speech to convince is used so widely that we are probably unaware of its frequency. Actually, very few persons do what someone else suggests unless they are convinced. The pattern of ideas employed in a speech to convince is not always known to the person who uses it, but generally the speaker uses certain techniques to gain conviction.

You will undoubtedly be asked many times in your life to present ideas and arguments. This speech assignment offers practice in the art of convincing an audience.

Explanation of the Speech to Convince

The speech to convince is one which causes your audience willingly to accept your proposal through logic, evidence, and emotion. You must present sufficient logic and evidence to swing the audience to your belief. This often means that you will also ask them to take the action you suggest. It is usually wise and necessary to appeal to emotions that accompany the attitudes and decisions you desire from your audience. These basic emotions may be reached by certain basic appeals, such as love of country, self-preservation, desire for recognition, desire for adventure, loyalty, political beliefs, religion, and the like. This necessitates a thorough analysis of your audience so that you may base your appeal on their beliefs and attitudes. It also means that you must present your logic and evidence in such a way that it will direct their thinking through channels they can readily follow.

The speech to convince is utilized on many kinds of occasions. At most popular gatherings — political meetings, lecture forums, charity drives, community drives, church services, and other civic gatherings — an effort is made to convince. Business meetings involve conviction any time differences of opinion prevail. Decisions are reached by convincing someone. Any time a debate is in progress — whether a formal argument between two rival schools, within a legislative body, among three farmers, or in court proceedings — the statements of the speakers involve persuasion through logic, evidence, and emotion.

Suggested Topics for Speeches to Convince

1. Eighteen years should be the national age limit for voting.
2. Every mentally able person should be legally compelled to attend school until he completes two years of high school.
3. All state colleges and universities should abolish fees.
4. No student should be permitted to carry more than . . . . semester hours of college work during any one semester.
5. Colleges should provide free yearbooks to all students.
6. Colleges should require all students to carry health insurance while enrolled.
7. All seniors with a four-year B average should be excused from final examinations.
8. Mercy killings should be legalized nationally.
9. Strikes should be prohibited by law.
10. Compulsory arbitration of all labor disputes should be established by law.
11. Gambling should be legalized nationally.
12. The feeble-minded should be sterilized.
13. Slot machines should be outlawed nationally.
14. College athletes should not be subsidized.
15. Women should be drafted into the armed services.
16. Capital punishment should be abolished nationally.
17. All known dope addicts should be committed to special hospitals for treatment.
18. The atomic bomb should be outlawed in war.
19. All high schools and colleges should have courses pertaining to marriage.
20. Speaker's choice of a controversial subject.

How to Choose a Topic

Study the suggestions; then make your choice on the basis of suitability to you, your audience, and the occasion. If you do not select one of the suggested topics, be extremely careful in choosing a topic of your own. Watch the way you word your topic and what you propose to convince your audience of. In wording your topic be sure you propose that your audience should adopt a certain debatable proposition. For example, you may decide to convince your listeners that "All school books should be free." Notice the word "should." It implies "ought to be." Your purpose is to persuade your audience to believe that this is a sound idea and will be beneficial if carried out. You are not asking them to carry it out by standing behind a book counter and handing out free text books.

A sales talk is not a speech to convince, because your purpose is to make your customer reach down in his pocket, pull out his money, and give some to you. This requires him to do something. Naturally a certain amount of convincing precedes your request for his money, but your actual purpose is to make him hand you a specific amount of money. You do not care whether he changes his mind or not, just so you get his money. We may conclude, then, that a speech to convince is not a sales talk, is not primarily to stimulate or arouse; it is one in which your purpose is to change a person's mind about something on which there is definite disagreement.

Your topic must be a proposition which is specific and which offers a debatable solution to a controversial problem. It is not adequate to propose the subject, "We should all drive more carefully." We agree on this already. To talk on such a broad topic would be merely to stimulate or arouse. (See the project covering the speech to stimulate or arouse.) If you wish to do something to make us more careful drivers, suggest a definite and debatable solution, such as: "The legislature should pass a law limiting speed on the highways to sixty miles per hour," or "All persons convicted of traffic violations should be compelled to attend a driver's school for two weeks." These are proposals about which people disagree. We can readily say *yes* or *no* to them. We can debate them, but we cannot debate the subject, "We should all drive more carefully," because we agree on it.

Examine your topic closely to be certain you have a correct one on which to base your speech to convince. If you are in doubt, consult your instructor.

How to Prepare a Speech to Convince

In preparing the speech to convince, remember that your purpose is to swing people over to your beliefs so that they not only will think what you want them to think, but will also do what you tell them to do. This is obviously not an easy task; however, it is not impossible. To achieve the "convincing effect," you need to look carefully into the organization of your speech. Briefly, it may be as follows; though all the suggested steps do not necessarily apply in all cases.

1. *Give a history of the problem.* Discuss the events leading up to the present time that make the topic important. Tell why it is significant that the audience hear the discussion you are about to present. (Do not spend too much time on the history; you have other points to cover.)

2. *Discuss the present-day effects of the problem.* Give examples, illustrations, facts, and views of authorities that clearly bring out the situation you are talking about. These are *musts* if you wish to be convincing.

3. *Discuss the factors that brought about the effects you listed in point 2.* Here again you must present examples, illustrations, facts, and views of authorities to prove your points. Be sure you show how these factors brought about the effects you mentioned.

4. *List possible solutions to the problem.* Discuss briefly the various alternatives that could be taken, but show that they are not effective enough to solve your problem. *Give evidence for your statements: examples, illustrations, authorities' views, facts and analogies.*

5. *Give your solution of the problem.* Show why your solution is the best answer to the proposition you are discussing. Present your evidence and the reason for believing as you do. This must not be simply your opinion. It must be logical reasoning backed up by evidence.

6. *Show how your proposal will benefit your audience.* This is the real meat of your entire speech, if you have completed each preceding step up to this point. Here is where you must convince. You definitely have to show your listeners how they will benefit from your proposal—for example, how they will make more money, be safer from an enemy, live longer, be

happier, get better roads, better schools, lower taxes, cheaper groceries. In other words, your listeners must see clearly and vividly that your proposal will help them. They must concur on this point.

7. *What, if anything, do you want your audience to do about the solution you propose?* Here is the proof of your effectiveness. You now tell your hearers what you want them to do. If you have been convincing up to this point, they will probably go along with you; if not, you have "stumbled" somewhere in your speech. You may ask the audience to write to their congressman, to vote for or against a bill, to give money to charity, to attend a rally, or to clean up their town. You suggest the action for them but you do not argue for its performance since this would lead into a speech to get action.

If you do not wish to follow the above procedure, here is one that accomplishes the same end but is described differently:

1. State your proposition in the introduction.
2. Give a history of the problem which brought up the proposal that you are asking be adopted.
3. Show that your proposal is *needed*. Offer evidence that establishes the *need* for *your* proposal. No other proposal (solution) will do.
4. Show that your proposition is *practical*. Give evidence to prove that it will *do* what you say it will. In other words, show that it will work.
5. Show that your proposition is *desirable*. Give evidence showing that what it will do will be *beneficial* rather than harmful. For example, concerning the desirability of military training people say, "Yes, military conscription will work, but it is *undesirable* because it will bring on militaristic control of our government."
6. Conclude your speech with a final statement in support of your proposal.

Note: If you are opposed to a certain proposal, you may establish your point of view by offering arguments which show any one of the following to be true:

1. The proposition is not needed. (Give evidence.)
2. The proposition is not practical. (Give evidence.)
3. The proposition is not desirable. (Give evidence.)

Of course, if you can establish all three of these points, you will be more convincing than if you prove only one.

You will face untold difficulty from your audience if you fail to have the body of your speech properly organized and all your points supported by evidence. The best guarantee of success is careful preparation. In addition to a well-organized speech with points supported by evidence, you must have a well-constructed introduction and a strong conclusion. However, even though you have volumes of evidence, clear-cut organization, and vivid language, you *must deliver the speech confidently and well*, without excessive use of notes, if anyone is to be convinced that you yourself are convinced about your own proposal.

Materials for preparing your speech can be secured from your library. Encyclopedias, Readers' Guides, magazine and newspaper indexes—all are excellent sources. Ask your instructor and librarian for assistance.

How to Present a Speech to Convince

In general, a frank, enthusiastic, and energetic presentation is desirable. A reasonable amount of emotion may be evident; however, it should not be overdone.

Your bodily action should suit the words you utter and be such an integral part of your overall presentation that no attention is directed toward it. Vigor and intensity should characterize your bodily action. Show by your actions that *you* are convinced.

Your voice should reflect sincere belief in your views and, through inflection and modulation, carry the ring of truth and personal conviction. Sufficient force should be utilized to convey sound and meaning to all who listen.

Naturally your presentation will vary according to the occasion, the size of the room, the acoustics, and the type of audience before whom you give your speech. You would not speak to a small group of businessmen in the same manner as you would address a large political gathering.

BIBLIOGRAPHY

Borchers & Wise, chaps. 8, 13.
Brigance, *Speech Comm.*, pp. 120-134.
Brigance, *Speech Comp.*, chap. 3.
Brigance & Immel, chaps. 13-20.
Bryant & Wallace, *Fund.*, chap. 8.
Bryant & Wallace, *Oral Comm.*, chaps. 9, 12.

Buehler, part 2, chap. 4.
Dolman, chaps. 11, 12.
Gray & Braden, chaps. 9, 11, 12.
Hibbitt, chaps. 23-30.
Miller, complete book.
Monroe, *Prin. & Types*, chap. 18.

Name . . . . Date . . . . .Type of speech . . . .

Specific purpose of this speech . . . .

. . . . .No. of sources required . . . . . .

Sentence outline: 75-150 words.   Time limit: 5-6 minutes.   Speaking notes: Preferably none.

TITLE

INTRODUCTION

BODY

CONCLUSION

INSTRUCTOR'S COMMENTS

Clarity of purpose . . . .

Gesture-action-eye contact . . . .

Language . . . .

Voice . . . .

Enthusiasm and vigor. . . . .

Self-confidence . . . .

Organization . . . .

Introduction and conclusion . . . .

Grade . . . .

(List sources on back of page as indicated)

PRINTED SOURCES OF INFORMATION

Give complete information for each source.

1. Author's name . . . .

   Title of article . . . .

   Book or magazine containing article . . . .

   . . . . Date of publication . . . .

   Chapters and/or pages containing material . . . .

2. Author's name . . . .

   Title of article . . . .

   Book or magazine containing article . . . .

   . . . . Date of publication . . . .

   Chapters and/or pages containing material . . . .

3. Author's name . . . .

   Title of article . . . .

   Book or magazine containing article . . . .

   . . . . Date of publication . . . .

   Chapters and/or pages containing material . . . .

INTERVIEW SOURCES OF INFORMATION

1. Name of person interviewed . . . . Date of interview . . . .

   His title, position, and occupation . . . .

   . . . .

   Why is he an authority on the subject? Be specific . . . .

   . . . .

2. Name of person interviewed . . . . Date of interview . . . .

   His title, position, and occupation . . . .

   . . . .

   Why is he an authority on the subject? Be specific . . . .

   . . . .

3. Name of person interviewed . . . . Date of interview . . . .

   His title, position, and occupation . . . .

   . . . .

   Why is he an authority on the subject? Be specific . . . .

   . . . .

PROJECT 16

THE HECKLING SPEECH

A speaker never knows when he will be heckled by persons in his audience. Sometimes heckling occurs when it is least expected. When it does come, a speaker should be ready to meet it, whether it be mild or boisterous. This project provides practice in speaking under the pressure of heckling from your audience.

Another reason why this assignment is given is that a student speaker often becomes aroused when under fire from his audience. He throws off his habitually meek speaking personality and suddenly faces his tormentors with a great surge of confidence and power -- something he always had but did not use. This is a good feeling and inspires confidence in a speaker. This project is intended primarily to make you aware of your latent powers of expression so that you will use them in forthcoming speeches.

Explanation of a Heckling Speech

A heckling speech is one that a speaker delivers while being subjected to heckling from his audience. Usually it supports or opposes a definite proposition. Normally the speaker's purpose is to convince. The purpose could be to inform or stimulate, but in both these types of speeches heckling is likely to be slight. The speaker selects one side of a contention which he will support and then does his best to justify his views. He presents argument and evidence that strengthen his stand. All the while he is doing this, the audience is free to heckle him in any way it sees fit. His problem is to control the volatile attention of his disturbing listeners, and at the same time successfully propound his ideas. It is necessary that he have positive self-control, retain his sense of humor, be fully prepared, and understand how to handle hecklers.

This type of speech is not encountered on any specific occasion. Heckling arises somewhat unexpectedly. A speaker should be ready for it at any time.

Suggested Topics for a Heckling Speech

You are to take a side on one of the following subjects or a similar one, and you are to uphold that side of the argument. Work out the actual statement of your proposition.

1. All colleges should establish R.O.T.C. units.
2. Third or fourth terms for Presidents should not be prohibited by law.
3. National marriage laws with a minimum age limit, a physical examination, and a waiting period after applying for a license should be established by Congress.
4. National prohibition should be established by law.
5. Hawaii should be granted statehood.
6. Colleges should allow students free choice of subjects.
7. Girls' dormitories should abolish "hours" for all girls.
8. The Communist party should be declared illegal in the United States.
9. War should be declared only by vote of a majority of the people.
10. The atomic bomb should be outlawed.
11. Hazing should be abolished on all college campuses.
12. College housing should be available for married students.
13. Married women with children under twelve years of age should be prohibited from gainful employment.
14. The student newspaper should have no faculty control.
15. The Student Council should try all discipline cases.
16. Athletes should not receive special help from the college.
17. National speed limits should be established for automobile drivers.
18. National driver's license requirements should be established.
19. Picketing should be prohibited in time of war.
20. Speaker's choice of a proposition.

How to Choose a Subject for a Heckling Speech

When studying the above list of propositions, visualize yourself as being for or against one of them. For this reason, select a subject upon which you hold a definite opinion and one which will require you to secure additional information.

How to Prepare for a Heckling Speech

The purpose of this particular heckling speech is to convince your audience. Because you know in advance that you will be heckled, your secondary purpose will be to control your audience and put your ideas across.

The organization of this speech should be modeled on that of any speech to convince. Reread Project 15 for information on organization. Besides having your sequence of ideas well in mind, know it so thoroughly that you cannot forget it. Under heckling pressure, loss of memory may be so overwhelming that you may stand blankly before your audience. If they can disturb you to this extent, they will be delighted. This speechlessness need not trouble you if you are prepared for many interruptions.

How to Present a Heckling Speech

Keep your head. Your attitude should be one of firmness and good humor, but not officiousness or haughtiness. Your good humor should not permit you to be so sensitive to its presence that you laugh or turn to histrionics every time someone shoots a question at you or puts you on the spot. Be sensitive to any situation that demands a witticism or similar response from you. Demonstrate enough flexibility in meeting your hecklers to display the basic qualities of poise and self-confidence.

Your audience will be greatly pleased if they can disturb you or cause you to become so confused that you forget your speech or fly off on a tangent, leaving your speech somewhere behind you. How can you avoid losing your poise? First of all, know your speech and know it well. Do not have a memorized talk, but have a memorized sequence of points which comprise your main ideas. Refuse to answer irrelevant questions that are nothing but quips, popoffs, or teasers. Simply state that such remarks are irrelevant, do not pertain to your speech, and hence cannot be answered. Whenever you are in doubt as to what your interrogator wants, ask him to repeat his question. A persistent heckler can sometimes be silenced by a quick retort to some of his senseless chatter.

Expect all kinds of interruptions, but do not be disturbed by them. If the questions are legitimate, clear them up or tell the group that you will answer a certain question later in your speech after you discuss the point that has just been brought up. *Before you end your remarks, draw your thoughts together with a good conclusion.*

Throughout your speech, talk clearly, forcefully, and correctly. Accompany your words with effective bodily actions and gestures. Look and act confident.

Special hints: (1) Be firm but flexible. (2) Retain a sense of humor but do not interpret everything as something to be handled as if you were a comedian. (3) Show no anger but do not be afraid to stand up and face your audience vigorously and forcefully. (4) Maintain self-control. (5) Take advantage of opportunities offered by events that occur while you speak. (6) Stay with your speech by refusing to be "jockeyed" out of position. (7) Do not ask questions or opinions of your hecklers when replying to them. They will only argue with you. Give short, direct, vigorous, and specific replies. (8) If a heckler is a constant irritant who just sits and makes noises which he thinks are questions, ask him directly to be quiet and give other people a chance. (9) When questions come fast and furiously, *point to one person* to ask his question while signaling for the others to be quiet so you can answer. Try to direct the audience's attention to the person who is questioning (and heckling). An audience will usually be courteous to one of its own members. This will give the speaker a chance. (10) Whenever the opportunity comes to flatten a heckler verbally, give him both barrels with a triple charge of powder. (11) Do not answer more than two questions at a time from one person. Give others a chance to be heard. (12) Do not argue with a heckler; switch to someone who has a question. (13) If the session gets too rough, frankly ask the audience to give you a chance -- appeal to their sense of fair play. (14) When the heckling gets loud, stop completely, *wait calmly until quiet returns*, then quietly and definitely answer a question or resume your speech. Do not attempt to talk louder than your heckler.

How to Heckle

Interrupt the speaker at will, either seated or standing up. Ask such questions as: How do you know? Who's your authority? Where did you read that? What do you mean? Will you please explain . . . . ? What is your evidence? Members of the audience may argue with the speaker (if he is naive enough to fall into such a trap.) Clever remarks about the speaker, what he is saying and/or doing are excellent heckling devices. Be a skillful heckler, not a boring one. "Getting the speaker's goat" is an effective method of heckling.

These practices *should not be overdone*. However, you as the audience are obliged to see that each speaker knows, when he has finished his speech, that he has been through the fire; otherwise his experience will be weakened. Applaud each speaker generously when he concludes.

BIBLIOGRAPHY

Hibbitt, pp. 125-126.
Monroe, *Prin. & Types*, chap. 19.

O'Neill & Weaver, chap. 24.
Thompson, pp. 11-16.

Name . . . . Date . . . . Type of speech . . . .

Specific purpose of this speech . . . .

. . . . .No. of sources required . . . . . .

Sentence outline: 75-150 words.   Time limit: 5-6 minutes.   Speaking notes: None.

TITLE

INTRODUCTION

BODY

CONCLUSION

INSTRUCTOR'S COMMENTS

   Clarity of purpose . . . .

   Gesture-action-eye contact . . . .

   Language . . . .

   Voice . . . .

   Enthusiasm and vigor . . . .

   Self-confidence . . . .

   Organization . . . .

   Introduction and conclusion . . . .

   Grade . . . .

             (List sources on back of page as indicated)

PRINTED SOURCES OF INFORMATION

Give complete information for each source.

1. Author's name . . . .
   Title of article. . . . .
   Book or magazine containing article . . . .
   . . . . Date of publication . . . .
   Chapters and/or pages containing material . . . .

2. Author's name . . . .
   Title of article. . . . .
   Book or magazine containing article . . . .
   . . . . Date of publication . . . .
   Chapters and/or pages containing material . . . .

3. Author's name . . . .
   Title of article. . . . .
   Book or magazine containing article . . . .
   . . . . Date of publication . . . .
   Chapters and/or pages containing material . . . .

INTERVIEW SOURCES OF INFORMATION

1. Name of person interviewed. . . . . Date of interview . . . .
   His title, position, and occupation . . . .
   . . . .
   Why is he an authority on the subject? Be specific. . . . .
   . . . .

2. Name of person interviewed. . . . . Date of interview . . . .
   His title, position, and occupation . . . .
   . . . .
   Why is he an authority on the subject? Be specific. . . . .
   . . . .

3. Name of person interviewed. . . . . Date of interview . . . .
   His title, position, and occupation . . . .
   . . . .
   Why is he an authority on the subject? Be specific. . . . .
   . . . .

THE SPEECH TO STIMULATE — ANY SUBJECT

People need to be stimulated or aroused if they are to be concerned about a proposition or problem that is laid before them. Often a speaker appeals to his audience to do something, to change their minds, to give consideration to an idea, but he does not stir them sufficiently to make them willing to be more than mildly interested. As a speaker it is to your advantage to learn the methods and approaches that cause audiences to be stimulated by speech. This assignment provides an experience for the speech to arouse or stimulate so that you will be fully aware of the importance of this type of speech.

Explanation of the Speech to Stimulate

The speech to stimulate an audience is one that does just that — it stimulates. Its purpose is to make people sharply aware of a problem, a condition, or a situation. They should be made to feel so concerned and stirred up about it that they want to do something to change and improve it. If its purpose is fulfilled, the speech touches the emotions and influences the intellect of the audience sufficiently that they feel impelled to adopt new attitudes and/or take action suggested by the speaker. The basic features of this speech are use of vivid language, obvious sincerity and enthusiasm on the part of the speaker, and appeals to basic drives that all persons have. Stimulation can be achieved by utilizing catchy slogans, concreteness, specific examples, illustrations, contrast, and facts.

Best-known occasions for the speech to stimulate are anniversaries, dedications, commencement exercises, religious gatherings, conventions, rallies, pep meetings, sales promotions, and between halves in a game when a coach arouses his men to a high pitch of fury accompanied by a will to win.

The speech demands that the speaker himself be aroused and vigorous. It calls for enthusiasm, energy, force, power, and spirit; the quantity and quality depend on the response sought from the audience. But most of all it requires that the speaker be sincere.

Suggested Topics for a Speech to Stimulate

These topics are only suggested. They are intended to give you a few ideas so that if you do not select one of them you may develop a topic of your own.
1. Narcotics -- our greatest enemy.
2. Unions -- a blessing or a curse.
3. We must learn to slow down and relax.
4. Education -- the way to liberty.
5. Everyone should vote.
6. Religion -- hope of mankind.
7. People are lazy.
8. Promotional meeting -- sales, political, sports, etc.
9. Peace -- the world's greatest need.
10. Any campaign -- Community Chest, Red Cross, Scout, Salvation Army, election, etc.
11. We should drive more carefully.
12. Our great political system -- safeguard or hazard.
13. Hurried marriages.
14. Careless hunters.
15. Cheaters on examinations.
16. Bribery in athletics.
17. Inflation is dangerous.
18. War -- the curse of mankind.
19. Crime -- our greatest threat.
20. Speaker's choice.

How to Choose a Topic

Regardless of what kind of speech you present, it should always possess sincerity. Of all the many kinds of speeches, none demands sincerity from the speaker more than the speech intended to stimulate or arouse. Therefore, in choosing a topic from the above list or in formulating your own, place sincerity foremost in your thinking. Do not try to find a subject that is suitable for Congress or for presentation over a national radio network. Find one suitable for your audience, in this case your classmates. It does not have to be something big, startling, or overwhelming. The speech should be appropriate to your situation and your audience, within the scope of your experience, and, above all, one in which you can be sincere.

How to Prepare a Speech to Stimulate

Basically, you will prepare this speech according to the steps followed in preparing any speech. It is essential that you give more than passing attention to your purpose -- to stimulate. This purpose will be behind every statement you utter, superimposed on your entire construction; hence, it must receive first consideration.

Having made yourself keenly aware of your purpose, set about achieving this purpose. Naturally, your attention turns to organization. We will assume that you have gathered your materials and are ready to arrange them in the various divisions of your outline. First, as always, think of your introduction. It may be that you will construct it or alter it after certain other parts of your speech are completed, but certainly you will give it close attention before you are ready to say that your speech is prepared. In arranging and organizing the main body of your remarks, your language undergoes no little scrutiny. Word pictures, graphic illustrations, all apt, must be presented with vivid phraseology that will call up definite associations in the minds of your listeners. You may also use slogans and catchy phrases to make your ideas remain with your hearers. Be concrete and specific by naming persons and places that the speech calls for. Avoid the abstract and intangible when giving examples, illustrations, and facts. This means not that you are to employ needless detail, but that your ideas must be aimed to hit their mark and make a strong impact. As stated above, you may use contrast as a means of clarifying your thoughts and pointing up their significance. Certainly throughout your entire speech you will appeal to the basic drives in people: security, saving or making money, keeping the home intact, gaining recognition, enjoying social position, having a cleaner city or town, knowing new experiences. In other words, you touch your listeners' pride, their pocketbooks and bank accounts, their sympathies, their family and home affections -- yes, even their fighting spirit. Once you have stimulated your audience, thoroughly aroused them, you can point out how their thinking or conduct may be affected by the ideas you are advancing. But the speech to impress does not call for action in the sense that you are asking for contributions, votes, etc.

How to Present a Speech to Stimulate

A forceful, dynamic, and energetic presentation should be used unless you are speaking on a solemn occasion calling for reverence, devotion, or deep feeling. In this case your voice and manner should be an animated and sincere projection of your ideas, accompanied by appropriate bodily action and gestures. But on other occasions you should show that you are alive with your subject, full of it, and eager for others to share it. Above all, you must be sincere and earnest. Remember that your audience will reflect your activity and eloquence. They will be just as lively or as solemn as you stimulate them to be.

BIBLIOGRAPHY

Borchers & Wise, chaps. 8, 13.
Brigance, *Speech Comm.*, chap. 4.
Brigance, *Speech Comp.*, chap. 3.
Brigance & Immel, chap. 13.

Gray & Braden, chaps. 4, 18.
Hibbitt, chaps. 23-30.
Monroe, *Prin. & Types*, chap. 17.
Thompson, part 2.

SPEECH OUTLINE, PROJECT 17

Name . . . . Date . . . . Type of speech . . . .

Specific purpose of this speech . . . .

. . . . No. of sources required . . . . . .

Sentence outline: 75-150 words.   Time limit: 4-5 minutes.   Speaking notes: Preferably none.

TITLE

INTRODUCTION

BODY

CONCLUSION

INSTRUCTOR'S COMMENTS

Clarity of purpose. . . . .

Gesture-action-eye contact . . . .

Language . . . .

Voice. . . . .

Enthusiasm and vigor . . . .

Self-confidence . . . .

Organization . . . .

Introduction and conclusion . . . .

Grade. . . . .

(List sources on back of page as indicated)

PRINTED SOURCES OF INFORMATION

Give complete information for each source.

1. Author's name ....
   Title of article..
   Book or magazine containing article ....
   .... Date of publication ....
   Chapters and/or pages containing material ....

2. Author's name ....
   Title of article..
   Book or magazine containing article ....
   .... Date of publication ....
   Chapters and/or pages containing material ....

3. Author's name ....
   Title of article..
   Book or magazine containing article ....
   .... Date of publication ....
   Chapters and/or pages containing material ....

INTERVIEW SOURCES OF INFORMATION

1. Name of person interviewed........................ Date of interview ....
   His title, position, and occupation ....
   ....
   Why is he an authority on the subject? Be specific.........................
   ....

2. Name of person interviewed........................ Date of interview ....
   His title, position, and occupation ....
   ....
   Why is he an authority on the subject? Be specific.........................
   ....

3. Name of person interviewed........................ Date of interview ....
   His title, position, and occupation ....
   ....
   Why is he an authority on the subject? Be specific.........................
   ....

PRESENTING A GIFT OR AWARD

Every time an occasion for presenting a gift or award occurs, someone must make the presentation speech. It is not easy to make a public presentation graciously and to utter thoughts that symbolize the spirit of the event. Yet at any time you may be designated to do this. Hence you should know something about making a presentation speech.

Explanation of the Presentation Speech

A presentation speech is short, sincere, and commendatory. It requires tact and good taste. Neither too much nor too little should be said about the recipient, especially if there has been intense rivalry in seeking the award. To understand the feeling of the audience, to avoid embarrassing the winner, and to use language appreciated by all or even the majority requires a simple but artistic quality of speech.

Occasions for this type of speech vary. A prize may have been won in a contest. Here the prize and perhaps the winner are known beforehand; for this reason there is no surprise element. At other times there will be expectancy, uncertainty, and even divided opinion among the judges regarding the winner. This poses a delicate problem for the speaker who makes the presentation. Emphasis will be placed upon interest, the careful consideration given by the judges, and their difficult position.

On another occasion an object is given to a person or an organization, such as a school, church, city, society, or other group. Here the whole atmosphere is formal. The procedures, plans, and persons who participate are known long before the actual donation takes place. There is no surprise. The speech is pointed to emphasize the symbolism or utility of the gift.

Still another occasion involves awarding a medal or other recognition for service. The surprise element may or may not be present. Depending on the occasion and the type of recognition, there may be much emotion. The ceremony and speech should not make it difficult for the recipient. The sentiment represented will obscure the gift itself, although tribute will be paid the one who is honored. During times of national crisis or emergency, frequent occasions arise for such presentations.

A fourth kind of award combines an award for services with a farewell. Surprise is often present. There is no rivalry, but rather good fellowship and possibly a little sadness. Occasions for this kind of award are the retirement of a president or other officer from a society, a school, or a civic organization, the leave-taking of a pastor, and the departure of any prominent citizen from community or group service. Here, emphasis is placed on the happy side of joyful fellowship. Some regret for the departure is expressed, but hope for the future is given a prominent place.

Suggested Types of Presentation Speeches

Construct a short speech for one of the following occasions:
1. Present an award to the head of a business firm.
2. Present an award to an employee with the longest tenure.
3. Present an award to a retiring school official.
4. Present a medal for outstanding leadership in the community.
5. Present a medal for outstanding achievement.
6. Present $5000 to the college to apply on a new building.
7. Present a set of books to a library.
8. Present a cash prize to the winner of a sales contest.
9. Present a cup to a beauty contest winner.
10. Present a scholarship of $100 to a college student.
11. Present an award to a minister who is leaving.
12. Present an award to the home-coming queen.
13. Present an award for making a new scientific discovery.
14. Present a medal for meritorious service during a flood.
15. Present a safe-driving award.

16. Present a swimming pool to a city.
17. Present an organ to a church.
18. Present a cup to the winner of a speech tournament.
19. Present a cash prize to a short-story contest winner.
20. Speaker's choice.

How to Choose a Topic

Study the above list carefully. The suggestions represent different occasions for gifts or awards. Choose one that you would like to use by visualizing the occasion and ceremony.

How to Prepare a Presentation Speech

In preparing this speech, make certain that you are fully aware of the occasion and any particular requirements governing it or the presentation. Keep in mind that it is an honor to present a gift or award; that it is not an opportunity to make a speech on your pet subject. By all means observe proper speech construction.

In preparing your talk, keep several predominating thoughts in mind. Do not overpraise the individual but pay deserving tribute to the recipient. Be careful not to overemphasize the gift or its value. Stress instead the work or honor which the award signifies. Let glory abide in achievement, not in the material object.

Briefly, your specific organization of ideas may fall into the following sequence: Make appropriate remarks to the audience; let these remarks refer to the occasion that brought the group together. Give a short history of the event that is now being fittingly culminated. State the immediate reasons for the award and show that, regardless of its value, it is only a token of the real appreciation of the service rendered or the esteem felt for the recipient.

As for the recipient, recount his personal worth and tell how it was recognized or discovered. If you know him personally, mention the fact that you are intimately aware of his service or merit.

Next, explain the character and purpose of the gift or award. Should it be a picture or statue, the custom is to have it veiled until the speech is concluded or nearly concluded and then at the proper moment withdraw the veil. If the gift or award is to be presented to an organization, be sure that someone is informed ahead of time that he is to represent it in receiving the gift.

How to Present a Presentation Speech

Be sure that the award or gift is available and ready to be presented. When the moment arrives for you to transfer it to the recipient, call him to the platform. If he is already on it, address him by name so that he may rise in response. Then, in a few properly chosen words, present the gift in summarizing the reasons for the presentation. Mention the appropriateness of the award and offer the recipient good wishes for the future. After he has accepted the award, give him time to thank you or make other remarks to you or to the people gathered around. An acceptance speech will be in order. Step back upstage and sit down while it is being delivered.

A few technicalities to observe are these: Be sure you stand so that the audience can see and hear you. Do not stand in front of the gift. Let the audience see it. Near the conclusion of your speech, when you are ready to make the presentation, pick up the gift or award, being particular to hold it so that it is clearly visible to everyone. Stand with your side turned slightly toward the audience. In giving the gift to the recipient, use the hand nearest him (the upstage hand). He will accept it with his upstage hand. If it is a medal you are to pin to his coat, stand with your side turned to the audience while pinning it on. Should the award be a picture, statue, or other object which cannot be transferred from hand to hand, it should be unveiled or shown at the moment of presentation.

BIBLIOGRAPHY

Baker, chap. 10.
Brigance, *Speech Comp.*, pp. 300-306.
Bryant & Wallace, *Fund.*, pp. 550-553.
Buehler, part 2, chap. 6.
Butler, chap. 7.

Crocker, *Pub. Spkg.*, chap. 22.
Glasgow, pp. 171, 172.
Hibbitt, pp. 205, 206.
Monroe, *Prin. & Types*, chap. 23.
O'Neill & Weaver, chap. 26.

Name . . . . Date . . . . .Type of speech . . . .

Specific purpose of this speech . . . .

. . . . .No. of sources required . . . . . .

Sentence outline: 50-75 words.   Time limit: 1-3 minutes.   Speaking notes: None.

TITLE

INTRODUCTION

BODY

CONCLUSION

INSTRUCTOR'S COMMENTS

   Clarity of purpose. . . . .

   Gesture-action-eye contact . . . .

   Language . . . .

   Voice. . . . .

   Enthusiasm and vigor . . . .

   Self-confidence . . . .

   Organization . . . .

   Introduction and conclusion . . . .

   Grade. . . . .
         (List sources on back of page as indicated)

PRINTED SOURCES OF INFORMATION

Give complete information for each source.

1. Author's name . . . .
   Title of article . . . .
   Book or magazine containing article . . . .
   . . . . Date of publication . . . .
   Chapters and/or pages containing material . . . .
2. Author's name . . . .
   Title of article . . . .
   Book or magazine containing article . . . .
   . . . . Date of publication . . . .
   Chapters and/or pages containing material . . . .
3. Author's name . . . .
   Title of article . . . .
   Book or magazine containing article . . . .
   . . . . Date of publication . . . .
   Chapters and/or pages containing material . . . .

INTERVIEW SOURCES OF INFORMATION

1. Name of person interviewed. . . . . .Date of interview . . . .
   His title, position, and occupation . . . .
   . . . .
   Why is he an authority on the subject? Be specific. . . . .
   . . . .
2. Name of person interviewed. . . . . Date of interview . . . .
   His title, position, and occupation . . . .
   . . . .
   Why is he an authority on the subject? Be specific. . . . .
   . . . .
3. Name of person interviewed. . . . . Date of interview . . . .
   His title, position, and occupation . . . .
   . . . .
   Why is he an authority on the subject? Be specific. . . . .
   . . . .

PROJECT 19

ACCEPTING A GIFT OR AWARD

Untold numbers of presentation speeches for gifts and awards are made every year; hence almost as many acceptance speeches are made by persons honored with awards. The recipient is not always told in advance that he is to be honored, so he may be embarrassed if he does not know how to accept the honor with simple sincerity. This project gives you a definite background for such an event; for this reason it is important.

Explanation of the Acceptance Speech

A speech made by the receiver of a gift or award is a sincere expression of his appreciation of the honor accorded him. It should establish him as a friendly, modest, and worth-while individual to whom the people may rightfully pay tribute for merit and achievement. Its purpose should be to impress the donors with his worthiness and to make them happy in their choice. To do this will demand a gentility and simplicity that spring naturally from his heart. This is no time for artificial or hollow remarks uttered by a shallow-thinking person.

In some instances no speech is necessary; the only essential is a pleasant "Thank you," accompanied by an appreciative smile. To do more than this when more is not appropriate is awkward. However, when a speech is in order, it must be propitious. The recipient himself must decide whether or not a speech is necessary.

Suggestions for Acceptance Speeches

1. Accept a retirement award.
2. As captain of your basketball team accept a championship award.
3. Accept an award for outstanding performance of duty.
4. Accept a prize for a new invention.
5. Accept a medal for rescuing a drowning person.
6. Accept a cup for the debate team or some other team.
7. Accept a donation of funds for the new ball park.
8. Accept a prize for winning a golf match.
9. Accept a cup for winning a swimming contest.
10. Accept a scholarship.
11. Accept an award for a baseball team which you represent.
12. Accept a prize for your college for winning a contest.
13. Accept an award for long service on a particular job.
14. Accept a medal for outstanding community service.
15. Accept a medal for saving a life.
16. Accept a new cabin for the Boy Scouts; you are a sponsor.
17. Accept a donation for a church.
18. Accept a prize for raising superior livestock.
19. Accept a prize for writing poetry.
20. Speaker's choice.

How to Prepare an Acceptance Speech

This speech will necessarily be impromptu on some occasions; hence little preparation can be made other than by formulating a basic pattern of ideas about which you will speak. If you are informed in advance that you are to receive a gift or award, you should certainly prepare a speech. In this case all the principles of good speech construction and organization should be followed. However, in either case, there are several important points to be noted: First, use simple language. Second, in your initial remarks express a true sense of gratitude and appreciation for the gift. If you are really surprised you may say so; however, the surprise must be genuine. If you are not surprised, omit any reference to your feeling. No one will be moved by an attempt at naivete. Next, modestly disclaim all the credit for winning the award. Give credit

(73)

to those who assisted you in any way, for without them you could not have achieved your success. Praise their cooperation and support. Do not apologize for winning. Do not disclaim your worthiness. Inasmuch as you were selected to receive a tribute, be big enough to accept it modestly and graciously, but don't grovel. Your next point may be an expression of appreciation for the beauty and significance of the gift. Its nature will determine what you say. Do not overpraise or overvalue it. Observe suitable restraint. In no manner should you express disappointment. Conclude your remarks by speaking of your plans or intentions for the future, especially as they may be connected with the award or gift or with work associated with it. In a final word you may repeat your thanks for the object or recognition.

How to Present an Acceptance Speech

Your attitude must be one of sincerity, friendliness, appreciation, modesty, and warm enthusiasm. Conceit and ego must be entirely lacking. You should be personal, if the award is for you. If you represent a group, use the pronoun "we" instead of "I."

When the donor speaks to you, either come to the platform or rise and step toward him if you are already on the platform. If you approach from the audience, come forward alertly, neither hurrying nor loitering. Let your bearing be one of appreciation for what is to come. On the platform, stand near the donor but avoid viewing the award anxiously or reaching for it before it is extended to you. Do not stand in front of it. In accepting the award stand slightly sideways toward the audience, reach for and take it with the hand nearest the donor (the upstage hand); in this way you will avoid reaching in front of yourself or turning your body away from the audience. After receiving the award, hold it so it remains in full view of the audience. If it is too large to hold, place it in an appropriate spot on the stage and step to one side and begin your speech; that is, if a speech is appropriate for the occasion. Face the audience while speaking. If you are sitting in the audience, carry the award in your hand when you return to your seat; do not stuff it into your pocket even though it is small.

Now as to the speech itself. Observe all the elements of acceptable stage presence. Be dressed appropriately, maintain an alert posture, speak clearly and distinctly and loudly enough to be heard by all. If your speech is impromptu, you will not be expected to have the fluency of one who has been forewarned. Let your manner express undeniable friendliness and appreciation for the honor accorded you. Sincerity is the most important quality of your speech. It must be evident in your voice, your bodily actions, your gestures, the expression on your face, everything about you. Do not be afraid of a little emotion; just control it so you won't be overcome by it. Make no apologies for your speaking. Avoid awkward positions that are indicative of too much self-consciousness. Do these things, and your acceptance speech will be genuine and applauded by all who see and hear you.

BIBLIOGRAPHY

Baker, chap. 11.
Brigance, *Speech Comp.*, pp. 300-306.
Bryant & Wallace, *Fund.*, pp. 553-554.
Bryant & Wallace, *Oral Comm.*, chap. 13.
Butler, chap. 7.

Crocker, *Pub. Spkg.*, chap. 22.
Hibbitt, pp. 205-206.
Monroe, *Prin. & Types*, chap. 21.
Monroe, *Prin.*, pp. 229-238.
O'Neill & Weaver, chap. 26.
Woolbert & Weaver, chap. 5.

Name . . . . Date . . . . Type of speech . . . .

Specific purpose of this speech . . . .

. . . . No. of sources required . . . . . .

Sentence outline: 50-75 words.   Time limit: 1-2 minutes.   Speaking notes: None.

TITLE

INTRODUCTION

BODY

CONCLUSION

INSTRUCTOR'S COMMENTS

Clarity of purpose . . . .

Gesture-action-eye contact . . . .

Language . . . .

Voice . . . .

Enthusiasm and vigor . . . .

Self-confidence . . . .

Organization . . . .

Introduction and conclusion . . . .

Grade . . . .
(List sources on back of page as indicated)

PRINTED SOURCES OF INFORMATION

Give complete information for each source.

1. Author's name . . . .

   Title of article . . . .

   Book or magazine containing article . . . .

   . . . . Date of publication . . . .

   Chapters and/or pages containing material . . . .

2. Author's name . . . .

   Title of article . . . .

   Book or magazine containing article . . . .

   . . . . Date of publication . . . .

   Chapters and/or pages containing material . . . .

3. Author's name . . . .

   Title of article . . . .

   Book or magazine containing article . . . .

   . . . . Date of publication . . . .

   Chapters and/or pages containing material . . . .

INTERVIEW SOURCES OF INFORMATION

1. Name of person interviewed. . . . . Date of interview . . . .

   His title, position, and occupation . . . .

   . . . .

   Why is he an authority on the subject? Be specific. . . . .

   . . . .

2. Name of person interviewed. . . . . Date of interview . . . .

   His title, position, and occupation . . . .

   . . . .

   Why is he an authority on the subject? Be specific. . . . .

   . . . .

3. Name of person interviewed. . . . . Date of interview . . . .

   His title, position, and occupation . . . .

   . . . .

   Why is he an authority on the subject? Be specific. . . . .

   . . . .

THE WELCOME SPEECH

A speech of welcome is of sufficient importance so that you should know how it is organized and what it should do. It occupies a high place in speech making; on its effectiveness hinges much of the success of public relations among groups. You may be asked to give a speech of welcome in your own community at any time. It would be unfortunate to have to refuse to assist in promoting good will because you do not know how to present a speech of welcome. This assignment shows you how to prepare and deliver a good speech of welcome.

Explanation of the Speech of Welcome

A speech of welcome is made to one or a group of individuals for the purpose of extending greetings and promoting friendship. The person being welcomed should be made to feel that he is sincerely wanted and that his hosts are delighted to have him with them. The warmest kind of hospitality should be expressed in the welcoming speech. Its genuineness should be so marked that the hearer feels a spirit of gladness because he is the guest of a gracious host. The speech is characterized by brevity, simplicity, geniality, and sincerity.

Occasions for the speech of welcome may be extremely varied. It may be a reception for a distinguished visitor, for a returning native son, or for a total stranger. It may welcome a citizen home from foreign travel, missionary work, diplomatic service, or a business enterprise. It may welcome a school official, new minister, or county officer. If an organization is being honored, the welcome may be to a delegation such as an advertisers' club, a Chamber of Commerce, a booster club, or a group of county, city, school, or community representatives. In some cases, the welcome may be extended as a special gesture to a conference or convention. Whatever the occasion, the speech of welcome plays a prominent part.

Suggested Speeches of Welcome

1. A Farm Bureau official stops in your community.
2. An organization holds a convention in your city.
3. A neighboring Chamber of Commerce is your guest.
4. A booster club visits your city.
5. The governor stops over a few days on state business.
6. A banquet is held for the new college president.
7. A new minister comes to town.
8. A successful diplomat pays your city a visit.
9. A stranger visits a local civic organization.
10. Welcome a distinguished visitor.
11. An important conference meets in your city.
12. A nearby city sends a delegation to study your community's excellent school system, water-works, fire department.
13. An advertisers' club comes to your community.
14. A neighboring city sends a friendly delegation.
15. The city manager visits your Chamber of Commerce.
16. The newly elected school superintendent arrives in your city.
17. A missionary returns from foreign service.
18. A prominent citizen returns from foreign travel.
19. A native son comes home.
20. Speaker's choice.

How to Choose a Speech of Welcome

Select the occasion that interests you most. Decide definitely what organization you will represent and what position you hold in it. Select one that you know something about or one about which you can secure information. Study the above list and make your choice, or plan your own occasion if none of the above suggestions suits you.

How to Prepare a Speech of Welcome

First, fix your purpose in mind: You are to make your guests glad to be here. They should admire your hospitality. Next, get your information and organize your speech. You may need to explain the organization you represent. If so, mention its character and the work it is doing; relate points of interest about it, including future plans. Pay a tribute to your guests for their work and tell of the advantages gained by their visiting you. Note who the guests are, where they come from, and whom they represent. Explain briefly what their coming means and comment on the common interests your organization has with them. Speak of the occasion, its present enjoyment and its future importance. Express anticipated pleasant associations and mutual benefits to be derived from the meeting. Invite your guests to feel fully at home in your community. Speak for those whom you represent.

Not all the above material is always needed in a speech of welcome. Use only that which is appropriate, and adjust it to meet the occasion, whether it involve an individual or a group of people.

Do not say too much or too little. Make your remarks brief and pertinent. Considerable thought and organization will be required for this.

How to Present a Speech of Welcome

Let the occasion govern your presentation. If it is formal, act and speak appropriately. If it is informal, adjust yourself and your remarks accordingly. In either case, be sincere and genuine. Feel what you say. Express to your guests a degree of hospitality and a warmth of welcome that they will remember, but do not overdo it. Express the same friendliness you do when you open the door of your home to a friend. Your language should be simple, vivid, and appropriate, and devoid of slang and redundancy.

BIBLIOGRAPHY

Baker, chap. 8.
Brigance, *Speech Comp.*, pp. 300-304.
Bryant & Wallace, *Fund.*, pp. 555-557.
Bryant & Wallace, *Oral Comm.*, chap. 13.
Buehler, part 2, chap. 6.

Hibbitt, pp. 206-207.
Monroe, *Prin. & Types*, chap. 21.
Monroe, *Prin.*, pp. 229-238.
Norvelle & Smith, p. 172.
O'Neill, chap. 12.
O'Neill & Weaver, chap. 26.

SPEECH OUTLINE, PROJECT 20

Name . . . . Date . . . . Type of speech . . . .

Specific purpose of this speech . . . .

. . . . .No. of sources required . . . . . .

Sentence outline: 50-100 words.   Time limit: 2-3 minutes.   Speaking notes: None.

TITLE

INTRODUCTION

BODY

CONCLUSION

INSTRUCTOR'S COMMENTS

Clarity of purpose. . . . .

Gesture-action-eye contact . . . .

Language . . . .

Voice. . . . .

Enthusiasm and vigor . . . .

Self-confidence . . . .

Organization . . . .

Introduction and conclusion . . . .

Grade. . . . .

(List sources on back of page as indicated)

PRINTED SOURCES OF INFORMATION

Give complete information for each source.

1. Author's name . . . .

   Title of article. . . . .

   Book or magazine containing article . . . .

   . . . . Date of publication . . . .

   Chapters and/or pages containing material. . . . .

2. Author's name . . . .

   Title of article. . . . .

   Book or magazine containing article . . . .

   . . . . Date of publication . . . .

   Chapters and/or pages containing material. . . . .

3. Author's name . . . .

   Title of article. . . . .

   Book or magazine containing article . . . .

   . . . . Date of publication . . . .

   Chapters and/or pages containing material. . . . .

INTERVIEW SOURCES OF INFORMATION

1. Name of person interviewed. . . . . Date of interview . . . .

   His title, position, and occupation . . . .

   . . . .

   Why is he an authority on the subject? Be specific. . . . .

   . . . .

2. Name of person interviewed. . . . . Date of interview . . . .

   His title, position, and occupation . . . .

   . . . .

   Why is he an authority on the subject? Be specific. . . . .

   . . . .

3. Name of person interviewed. . . . . Date of interview . . . .

   His title, position, and occupation . . . .

   . . . .

   Why is he an authority on the subject? Be specific. . . . .

   . . . .

PROJECT 21

THE RESPONSE TO A WELCOME SPEECH

Organizations of most types meet on some occasions when visitors are present. Sometimes members of a national fraternal group just drop in. At other times the guests represent a similar organization, or they are attending a convention at which a certain society is host. The visitors are often welcomed by a speech, and it is natural that a response to the welcome be made. The purpose of this assignment is to acquaint you with this type of speech.

Explanation of the Response to a Welcome

Occasions for the speech in response to a welcome may arise any time a welcome is given, although a speech in response is not always necessary. These occasions may occur at conventions, at meetings of civic, religious, educational, fraternal, or business organizations, and the like.

The speech in response to a welcome is simply a reply to the felicitations expressed by the host. Its purpose is to cement good will and friendship, and to express the feelings that exist between the groups. It is short, brief, courteous, and friendly. Often it is impromptu — which places a burden of some fast thinking and logical talking on the person who presents it. It also demands sincerity and cordiality of manner from the speaker. This implies ability and art in the speaking process.

Suggested Speeches of Response

1. You are a pharmacy student visiting a pharmacy club. Respond to their welcome.
2. You are a drama representative at a convention. Respond to a welcome for all the representatives.
3. You are a new citizen. Respond to a welcome for newcomers at a dinner.
4. Visit a business similar to your own. Respond to the board of directors.
5. You are a debater at a tournament. Respond for your squad.
6. You visit a neighboring school athletic council. Respond.
7. You are a government official. Respond to a Farm Bureau welcome.
8. You are chief of police new to a city. Respond to your welcome by a civic organization.
9. You are with a booster train. Respond to your welcome.
10. Respond to a Rotary Club welcome.
11. Visit a foreign country. Respond to a welcome at one of their schools.
12. You join a new organization. Respond to their welcome.
13. You are a new church member. Respond to a welcome at a dinner.
14. Visit a new chapter of your fraternity. Respond to the president.
15. You are a professor visiting another college. Respond to the dean's welcome.
16. You are a student at a religious convention. Respond for your school.
17. You are a visiting student. Respond to a student council welcome.
18. You are a mayor visiting another city. Respond.
19. Respond to a Lions Club welcome, or one from any other civic organization.
20. Speaker's choice.

How to Choose a Topic for a Response Speech

If you have been in a situation similar to one of those mentioned above, why not select it for your response? If not, choose a situation that you believe you would enjoy. Your choice should hold an interest for you, regardless of how apathetic you may be at the moment.

How to Prepare a Speech of Response

First, keep in mind the purpose of your talk, namely, to express your appreciation of the hospitality extended you and to strengthen mutual feelings of friendship. Second, follow the principles of good speech construction. Include an introduction and conclusion. Make your speech brief.

In general, make the occasion for the welcome overshadow your own personality. Compliments proffered you may be adroitly directed to the occasion. More specifically, your remarks may be developed in the following manner. Address the host and those associated with him; acknowledge his welcome and the hospitality of the organization; and express sincere thanks for their courtesies. Extend greetings from your organization and show how the occasion is mutually advantageous to your host and your own group. Explain briefly what your organization is, what it stands for. Mention the benefits to be derived from the attitudes of mutual helpfulness and enjoyment which are evident at this meeting. Predict future pleasant associations with your host's organization; show that this acquaintance is only the beginning of long-lasting cooperation and friendship. Mention in conclusion that you have been made to feel most welcome and at home. Thank your hosts again for their hospitality, extend your best wishes, and be seated.

This speech may have to be impromptu. Because of the frequent possibility of impromptu speeches of response, set up a basic sequence of ideas which you can use in replying to any speech of welcome. If you are designated ahead of time to present this speech, you should organize and rehearse your speech carefully until you have it well in mind.

How to Present a Response Speech

Your attitude and demeanor must be a happy combination of appreciation and friendliness. Your remarks must have the qualities of sincerity and gratitude. The only way to attain these ends is to demonstrate them through appropriate bodily actions and simple understandable language.

When you are presented by your host, rise politely, smile pleasantly, and begin to speak. Avoid scraping your chair if you are at a table, or playing with the silverware in front of you. Maintain your poise by observing alert posture. Be brief, but do not give the appearance of having nothing to say. When you have finished your speech, sit down. Remember that you are still being observed.

Here are a few additional suggestions.

Be sure that your speech is appropriate to the audience and the occasion. Adjust your conduct in accordance with whether the occasion is formal or informal. Include a few serious thoughts in your speech, even though gaiety fills the air. Do not resort to telling only a series of stories or anecdotes. Do not apologize or act surprised. You should know that as a guest you are subject to being called upon at any time. Accept your responsibility and meet it like a mature person, by having something worth while to say

BIBLIOGRAPHY

Baker, chap. 9.

Borchers & Wise, chap. 13.

Brigance, *Speech Comp.*, pp. 300-305.

Brigance, *Spoken Word*, chap. 7.

Bryant & Wallace, *Fund.*, pp. 557-560.

Bryant & Wallace, *Oral Comm.*, chap. 13.

Norvelle & Smith, p. 172.

O'Neill & Weaver, chap. 26.

SPEECH OUTLINE, PROJECT 21

Name . . . . Date . . . . Type of speech . . . .

Specific purpose of this speech . . . .

. . . . No. of sources required . . . . . .

Sentence outline: 40-75 words.   Time limit: 1-2 minutes.   Speaking notes: None.

TITLE

INTRODUCTION

BODY

CONCLUSION

INSTRUCTOR'S COMMENTS

Clarity of purpose . . . .

Gesture-action-eye contact . . . .

Language . . . .

Voice . . . .

Enthusiasm and vigor . . . .

Self-confidence . . . .

Organization . . . .

Introduction and conclusion . . . .

Grade . . . .

(List sources on back of page as indicated)

PRINTED SOURCES OF INFORMATION

Give complete information for each source.

1. Author's name . . . .
   Title of article. . . . .
   Book or magazine containing article . . . .
   . . . . Date of publication . . . .
   Chapters and/or pages containing material . . . .

2. Author's name . . . .
   Title of article. . . . .
   Book or magazine containing article . . . .
   . . . . Date of publication . . . .
   Chapters and/or pages containing material . . . .

3. Author's name . . . .
   Title of article. . . . .
   Book or magazine containing article . . . .
   . . . . Date of publication . . . .
   Chapters and/or pages containing material . . . .

INTERVIEW SOURCES OF INFORMATION

1. Name of person interviewed. . . . . Date of interview . . . .
   His title, position, and occupation . . . .
   . . . .
   Why is he an authority on the subject? Be specific. . . . .
   . . . .

2. Name of person interviewed. . . . . Date of interview . . . .
   His title, position, and occupation . . . .
   . . . .
   Why is he an authority on the subject? Be specific. . . . .
   . . . .

3. Name of person interviewed. . . . . Date of interview . . . .
   His title, position, and occupation . . . .
   . . . .
   Why is he an authority on the subject? Be specific. . . . .
   . . . .

PROJECT 22

THE FAREWELL SPEECH

You may find yourself the guest of honor at a farewell party given by your business or social friends; or they may simply call a group together as a final gesture of esteem and admiration for you. The guest of honor is invariably asked to say a few words of farewell. Too often what he says may be only a mumble of incoherent remarks because he has never before had an experience of this kind and does not know what is appropriate. This speech assignment will point the way when you are called upon to make a farewell speech.

Explanation of the Farewell Speech

A farewell speech is one in which a person publicly says goodbye to a group of acquaintances. It should express the speaker's appreciation for what they have helped him accomplish and for the happiness they have brought him. It may be given at a formal or informal gathering, a luncheon or a dinner. Frequently on this occasion the guest of honor receives a gift from the group. Often an informal party occurs when "the boss," a superior, or some other leader calls a meeting following the day's work, at which time the person who is leaving will receive commendation, favorable testimonials, and possibly a gift. He too will be expected to "say something." The formal occasion is, of course, much more elaborate.

Occasions for the farewell speech are of one general kind — leave taking. Situations vary greatly; however, a few of the usual ones are the following: retiring after years of service in a certain job; taking a new job; being promoted to a different type of work that demands a change in location; concluding one's service with a civic or religious organization; leaving school; or moving to another community regardless of reason.

The occasion, whatever its nature, should not be treated with too much sadness. It should be approached with true sincerity and honesty. Feelings of deep emotion may be present; if so, they should be expressed in a manner in keeping with the occasion and everyone present.

Suggested Occasions for a Farewell Speech

1. Leaving on a rocket for the moon.
2. Going to New York to become an actor.
3. Leaving for South America to hunt oil.
4. Going on a two-year tour around the world.
5. Just married -- moving away.
6. Going back home after completing a year's job.
7. Retiring from a church position.
8. Taking a new job many miles away.
9. Joining the armed services.
10. Leaving school — a banquet for college seniors.
11. Going to Central America to survey jungle lands.
12. Leaving for the South Pole on a trip of exploration.
13. Going to Africa to do research on tropical diseases.
14. Going to Hollywood to try your hand at motion pictures.
15. Leaving a community where you were "stationed" on a job.
16. Retiring from a civic position.
17. Retiring from employment after twenty years.
18. Moving to a new location for any reason.
19. Going to college in a foreign country.
20. Speaker's choice.

How to Choose a Topic

First of all, is there any one of these topics that really compels your interest? If so, select it. If not, choose the one that interests you most, or think of similar situations and formulate your own topic.

How to Prepare a Farewell Speech

Remember that this is a special occasion and that old friends are honoring you. There may be an atmosphere of considerable sentiment and emotion or merely friendly gaiety. This means that you must carefully analyze your audience, their probable mood, and the general atmosphere. If you are likely to be presented with a gift, plan your remarks so that you will accept it graciously. Sincerity must dominate your utterances whatever they may be.

Farewell speeches usually follow a well-defined pattern with appropriate variations as the speaker deems necessary. It is advisable to begin your talk by referring to the time when you first arrived and why you came to the community. A bit of humor or some interesting anecdotes may be in good taste. The way you were welcomed or made to feel at home is an excellent recollection. Continue by pointing out how your ideals and those of your listeners, though not completely attained, inspired you to do what you did, that work remains still to be done. Express appreciation for their support of your efforts which made your achievements possible. Commend the harmony and cooperation that prevailed. Say that you will always remember your associations with this group as one of the outstanding events in your life. Speak of your future work briefly but sincerely. Explain why you are leaving, and what compelled you to go into a new field or location. Show that the work just completed will be a background and inspiration for what lies ahead. Continue by encouraging those who remain, predict greater achievements for them, praise your successor if you know who he is, and conclude with a genuine expression of your appreciation for them and continued interest in their future. If you received a gift, express a final word of thanks for it.

In your speech omit all references to any unpleasantnesses and friction that may have existed. Do not make the occasion bitter or sad. Be happy and leave others with the same feeling. Smile. Make sure that a good impression follows you.

How to Present a Farewell Speech

In this speech, fit your manner to the mood of the occasion and the audience. Do not go overboard in solemnity, emotion, or gaiety. Be appropriate. Use a friendly and sincere approach throughout. Adjust your introductory remarks to the prevailing mood; then move into your speech. Be sure that your language is appropriate to the five requirements just listed. Avoid ponderous phrases, overemotionalized words and tones, redundancy, and flowery attempts at oratory. Let everything you do and say, coupled with good appearance and alert posture, bear evidence that you are genuinely and sincerely mindful of your listeners' appreciation of you on your departure.

BIBLIOGRAPHY

Baker, chap. 19.
Borchers & Wise, chap. 13.
Brigance, *Speech Comp.*, pp. 300-307.
Hibbitt, pp. 206-207.

Monroe, *Prin. & Types*, chap. 23.
Monroe, *Prin.*, pp. 229-241.
O'Neill, chap. 12.
O'Neill & Weaver, chap. 26.

SPEECH OUTLINE, PROJECT 22

Name . . . . Date . . . . Type of speech . . . .

Specific purpose of this speech . . . .

. . . . .No. of sources required . . . . . .

Sentence outline: 75-100 words.   Time limit: 4-5 minutes.   Speaking notes: None.

TITLE

INTRODUCTION

BODY

CONCLUSION

INSTRUCTOR'S COMMENTS

   Clarity of purpose . . . .

   Gesture-action-eye contact . . . .

   Language . . . .

   Voice . . . .

   Enthusiasm and vigor . . . .

   Self-confidence . . . .

   Organization . . . .

   Introduction and conclusion . . . .

   Grade . . . .

(List sources on back of page as indicated)

PRINTED SOURCES OF INFORMATION

Give complete information for each source.

1. Author's name . . . .

   Title of article. . . . .

   Book or magazine containing article . . . .

   . . . . Date of publication . . . .

   Chapters and/or pages containing material . . . .

2. Author's name . . . .

   Title of article. . . . .

   Book or magazine containing article . . . .

   . . . . Date of publication . . . .

   Chapters and/or pages containing material . . . .

3. Author's name . . . .

   Title of article. . . . .

   Book or magazine containing article . . . .

   . . . . Date of publication . . . .

   Chapters and/or pages containing material . . . .

INTERVIEW SOURCES OF INFORMATION

1. Name of person interviewed. . . . . Date of interview . . . .

   His title, position, and occupation . . . .

   . . . .

   Why is he an authority on the subject? Be specific. . . . .

   . . . .

2. Name of person interviewed. . . . . Date of interview . . . .

   His title, position, and occupation . . . .

   . . . .

   Why is he an authority on the subject? Be specific. . . . .

   . . . .

3. Name of person interviewed. . . . . Date of interview . . . .

   His title, position, and occupation . . . .

   . . . .

   Why is he an authority on the subject? Be specific. . . . .

   . . . .

PROJECT 23

THE EMOTIONAL SPEECH

The emotional speech is frequently delivered under intense emotional strain. Sometimes the intensity of the speaker and/or the audience is so pronounced that the speaker actually loses control of himself. To be most effective, a person should be capable of retaining self-control while experiencing deep emotion. One who finds himself suddenly undergoing personal emotion in a speech situation is at a real disadvantage. This speech assignment will provide training in the emotionally loaded speech.

Explanation of the Emotional Speech

An emotional speech is one dealing with an emotional subject. It may be that the occasion calls for emotion, or it may be that the audience is not aroused and will have to be talked to in a manner that will cause them to listen willingly and to accept a speech that has emotional content and delivery. Such a speech situation demands that the speaker be aroused to an emotional pitch commensurate with the reaction he wishes the audience to have. The listeners in turn will have to be fully convinced of the speaker's sincerity before they will permit themselves to feel a corresponding emotion. The point is this: If the audience is to be emotionally stimulated, the speaker must experience active emotions similar to those he wishes to arouse.

The purpose of an emotional speech is, of course, to arouse an audience emotionally; however, the specific feelings or emotions to be stimulated should be determined in advance by the speaker. Once the audience is sufficiently stimulated, he should be prepared to direct the emotions into the channels he desires.

A special feature of the emotional speech is the emphasis to be placed on certain emotions to bring about planned responses. Actually, the emotional speech could easily be classified as one intended to stimulate or arouse. In the emotional speech, however, the speaker plans to induce emotional feelings somewhat different from those described in the project on the speech to stimulate or arouse.

Occasions for emotional speeches arise at religious services, funerals, gatherings where tributes are paid, and certain school functions, especially those near the end of the school year. Civic organizations, fraternities, sororities, honorary clubs, and many others employ rituals involving emotional speeches and ceremonies. Patriotic and political gatherings are often brought to an end with speeches that are highly emotionalized. A wild type of emotional abandon is evinced at athletic rallies, football and basketball games, and similar events. Professional wrestling and boxing matches bring out primitive emotional displays from bystanders which often seem to border on hysteria. People leap to their feet, cry for blood, gesticulate crazily, all the while making speeches which do not bear printing.

It is obvious that situations involving emotional speeches are many. The thing to remember is that the speech, action, and mood must fit the occasion, the speaker, the audience, and the surroundings.

Suggestions for Emotional Speeches

Some types of feelings that may be aroused are:

1. Sympathy
2. Sorrow or grief
3. Remorse
4. Sadness
5. Anguish
6. Pity
7. Compassion
8. Hatred
9. Anger
10. Reverence
11. Patriotism
12. Resentment

Situations involving one or more of the following may be the basis for an emotional speech:

1. Sickness
2. Family separation
3. Disappointment
4. Goodbye
5. Adversity
6. Politics
7. Sacrifice
8. Patriotism
9. Little children
10. Cruelty
11. Suffering
12. Harshness
13. Abuse
14. Injustice
15. Death

How to Choose a Topic for an Emotional Speech

Decide on the basic emotion or feeling that you wish to arouse in your audience. Then decide on the situation you want to use to arouse it. For example, if you wish to stir up sadness and hatred, talk about little children killed by drunken drivers.

How to Prepare an Emotional Speech

Know what you want from your audience and organize your speech to get it. This means that you must decide what emotions you wish to arouse; that you will gather evidence and data to prove the points you are making. Having established the validity of your arguments, point out the significance and meaning of your evidence to your audience. As far as possible, relate the evidence to your listeners and show how they are vitally concerned. You may accomplish this by using examples, illustrations, analogies, and quotations, either poetry or prose. These devices should be striking, pathetic, sorrowful, or vivid, and typical of the point you are making. They should be carefully selected for their appropriateness and poignancy. If you are speaking about the horrible slaughter of little children each year by drunken drivers, give examples and instances where children have been killed. Use examples familiar to the audience. Show how their children may be next. Describe the grief-stricken families of the dead children. Talk about the happy children who were at play only yesterday and the lives they might have enjoyed. Finally, make your appeal for safer driving, if that is the appeal you wish to make. To refresh your memory on the stimulating and arousing aspects of this speech, study the project dealing with the speech to stimulate or arouse.

Having organized and arranged your speech so that it is as effective as you can make it, your next step is wording it. This may be done by rehearsing from a detailed outline or by writing the speech out in full. Regardless of which method you use, do not memorize your speech word for word; memorize only the sequence of ideas, and then rehearse the speech until you have mastered the content and feel ready to present it without notice. Be sure that the beginning and end of the speech are carefully prepared to introduce and conclude your thoughts effectively.

How to Present an Emotional Speech

This is a speech that demands great consistency from the speaker if he is to mean what he says. He must be deeply in earnest, very sincere, and personally aroused. His voice, gestures, bodily actions, and words must all emphasize his thought and mood. This implies suitable bodily action, a variable speaking rate, grave tones, deliberation, and evidence of deep emotion, *under control*. There may well be an impression that the speaker is repressing pent-up feelings. Dignity and poise are invaluable in a speech of this kind. The energy and power in the entire speech should be so strongly marked that their force is unmistakable.

To attain the above presentation a speaker will be wise to begin his remarks calmly and without haste. As he progresses he may increase his tempo and vary his mood accordingly. A well-planned beginning and ending will lend untold emphasis.

BIBLIOGRAPHY

Crocker, *Pub. Spkg.*, pp. 152-154, 303-307.
Monroe, *Prin. & Types*, chap. 17.
O'Neill, pp. 80-88.

Sarett & Foster, pp. 112, 113, 223-225.
Thonssen & Gilkinson, pp. 327-330, 509.
Weaver, chap. 15.

Name . . . . Date . . . . Type of speech . . . .

Specific purpose of this speech . . . .

. . . . No. of sources required . . . . . .

Sentence outline: 75-100 words.   Time limit: 5-6 minutes.   Speaking notes: None.

TITLE

INTRODUCTION

BODY

CONCLUSION

INSTRUCTOR'S COMMENTS

   Clarity of purpose . . . .

   Gesture-action-eye contact . . . .

   Language . . . .

   Voice . . . .

   Enthusiasm and vigor . . . .

   Self-confidence . . . .

   Organization . . . .

   Introduction and conclusion . . . .

   Grade . . . .

(List sources on back of page as indicated)

PRINTED SOURCES OF INFORMATION

Give complete information for each source.

1. Author's name . . . .
   Title of article. . . . .
   Book or magazine containing article . . . .
   . . . . Date of publication . . . .
   Chapters and/or pages containing material . . . .
2. Author's name . . . .
   Title of article. . . . .
   Book or magazine containing article . . . .
   . . . . Date of publication . . . .
   Chapters and/or pages containing material . . . .
3. Author's name . . . .
   Title of article. . . . .
   Book or magazine containing article . . . .
   . . . . Date of publication . . . .
   Chapters and/or pages containing material . . . .

INTERVIEW SOURCES OF INFORMATION

1. Name of person interviewed. . . . . Date of interview . . . .
   His title, position, and occupation . . . .
   . . . .
   Why is he an authority on the subject? Be specific . . . .
   . . . .
2. Name of person interviewed. . . . . Date of interview . . . .
   His title, position, and occupation . . . .
   . . . .
   Why is he an authority on the subject? Be specific . . . .
   . . . .
3. Name of person interviewed. . . . . Date of interview . . . .
   His title, position, and occupation . . . .
   . . . .
   Why is he an authority on the subject? Be specific . . . .
   . . . .

THE EULOGY

Frequently a person is called upon to eulogize or praise someone. There are several ways to do this. The type of eulogy you may be asked to present will of course depend on different aspects of the speech situation. But whatever that requirement may be, you will be better prepared to do a creditable job if you have had previous experience.

Explanation of the Eulogy

The eulogy is a speech of praise in honor or commemoration of someone living or dead. Sometimes eulogies are even presented for animals, particularly dogs and horses. A more fanciful and imaginative eulogy would be for inanimate objects, such as the sea or the mountains. Some eulogies are written for trees and flowers, and these too are abstract and fanciful in nature.

The purpose of a eulogy is to praise and evaluate favorably; it commends the finer qualities and characteristics of the subject eulogized. It stresses the personality of the person (or thing) concerned; it tells of his greatness and achievements, his benefit to society, and his influence upon people. It is not merely a simple biographical sketch of someone.

Occasions for eulogies are many. For living persons such a speech may be given on a birthday, at a dinner, at the dedication of a project someone has created and/or donated. Eulogies are often given on the formal announcement of a political candidate or at an inauguration. For persons who are dead, eulogies are offered on birthday anniversaries or in connection with notable events or achievements in their lives. Sometimes eulogies in the form of character studies are presented as an evidence of good living; these become lessons of life.

Suggestions for Eulogies

1. Samuel Gompers.
2. Alexander Graham Bell.
3. Booker T. Washington.
4. Henry Ward Beecher.
5. Dwight D. Eisenhower.
6. Herbert Hoover.
7. Franklin Delano Roosevelt.
8. Winston Churchill.
9. Douglas MacArthur.
10. Horace Greeley.
11. Woodrow Wilson.
12. Louis Pasteur.
13. William Jennings Bryan.
14. Ralph Waldo Emerson.
15. William Allen White.
16. Albert Einstein.
17. A friend.
18. A buddy.
19. A relative.
20. Speaker's choice.

How to Select a Person to Eulogize

Because your eulogy must be completely sincere, choose for it someone whom you greatly admire and who, in your opinion, is leading or has led a commendable life. Select someone about whom you can secure adequate information. Do not choose a classmate or the town loafer, in the belief that your choice will be clever or smart — you will only embarrass your classmate and make yourself appear immature. Think twice before deciding to eulogize a tree, the sea, or the mountains, a dog, horse, or other animal, because these are more difficult to eulogize than people. For the sake of experience, select a person as a subject for your eulogy.

How to Prepare a Eulogy

The purpose of a eulogy is set, regardless of the time, place, or occasion, because eulogies are intended to stimulate an audience favorably toward the subject and to inspire them to nobler heights by virtue of the examples set by the persons being praised.

Having selected the person to be eulogized, decide upon the method you will use in developing the eulogy. Your method and whether or not the individual is living will determine the material that is necessary. Let us examine several different methods of constructing a eulogy.

First, you may follow a *chronological order*, that is, take up events in the order of their occurrence or development. This will permit a study of the growth and orderly evolution of character in your subject. As you touch upon these broad and influential events in his life, point to them as evidences of (1) what he accomplished, (2) what he stood for, (3) the nature of his influence upon society, and (4) his probable place in history. In building your speech chronologically do not compose a simple biographical sketch. If you do, you will have an informative speech but not a eulogy. You must state how he reacted to the events in his life and what happened as a result of them. For example, if you were eulogizing Franklin D. Roosevelt (chronologically), you would recount, as one event, how he was stricken with infantile paralysis when a grown man, but you would not merely make a statement regarding the tragedy that befell him and then go on. Rather, you would show how his illness became a challenge to him, how he resolved to live a great life despite a pair of useless legs, how he overcame his handicap. You would show that, as a result of his sickness, he became more resolute, more determined, more kindly, and that today the nation honors him on his brithday and contributes millions of dollars to the fund to aid children afflicted with infantile paralysis. Other incidents should be given similar treatment.

A second method of developing a eulogy might well be called the *period method*. It covers the individual's growth by treating different periods in his life. It is very broad and makes no attempt to enumerate the many events of his life and their significance. Instead of this, using Franklin D. Roosevelt again as an example, you could speak of him as he went through (1) boyhood, (2) college life, (3) early political life, (4) late political life. In following this method you attempt to bring out the same basic points mentioned above, namely, (1) what he accomplished, (2) what he stood for, (3) his influence upon society. (4) his probable place in history. Although this treatment is broad, it can be quite effective.

Regardless of which method you use, there are certain necessary points to be observed. First, omit the unimportant events, the small things, and the insignificant details. Second, point up the struggles your subject made in order to achieve his aims; avoid overemphasis and exaggeration. Third, show the development of his ideas and ideals. Fourth, describe his relations and services to his fellow men and indicate their significance.

It is not necessary to cover up the faults of an individual; rather, admit the human element in him, neither dwelling on nor apologizing for it. It can be shown that despite weaknesses or shortcomings a man was great. But whatever the qualities of your subject, be honest in your treatment of him. It is only fair to assume that the good in him outweighed the bad by far, or you would not have elected to eulogize him.

In constructing your speech, pay careful attention to your introduction and conclusion. Aside from these, do not neglect the logical organization and arrangement of the remainder of your talk. Actually, a eulogy is a difficult speech to prepare. However, if you know what you wish to put into it, you should have no particular trouble.

Materials for eulogies may be found in *Who's Who*, histories, biographies, autobiographies, encyclopedias, newspapers, magazines, and similar sources. Consult your librarian for assistance.

How to Present a Eulogy

Your overall attitude must be one of undoubted sincerity. You must be a true believer in the man about whom you speak. Aside from your attitude, you will, of course, observe all the requirements of a good speech. There should be no showiness or gaudiness in your presentation that will call attention to you instead of your ideas about the subject of your speech.

You will need to be fully aware of the occasion and atmosphere when you deliver the eulogy. It is your responsibility to know what will be required of you in the way of carrying out rituals or ceremonies if they are part of the program. Since you will be in the limelight, you should fit easily into the situation without awkwardness. Naturally you must adjust your bodily actions and gestures to your environment and your audience. If you are sincere and well prepared, and mean what you say, the eulogy you present should be inspirational to all who hear it.

BIBLIOGRAPHY

Borchers & Wise, chap. 13.
Brigance, *Speech Comp.*, pp. 312-322.
Crocker, *Pub. Spkg.*, chap. 22.
Hibbitt, pp. 207-208.

Monroe, *Prin. & Types*, chap. 23.
Norvelle & Smith, chaps. 3, 14.
O'Neill, pp. 341-355.
O'Neill & Weaver, chap. 30.
Woolbert & Weaver, chap. 5.

SPEECH OUTLINE, PROJECT 24

Name . . . . Date . . . . Type of speech . . . .

Specific purpose of this speech . . . .

. . . . No. of sources required . . . . . .

Sentence outline: 75-100 words.   Time limit: 5-6 minutes.   Speaking notes: None.

TITLE

INTRODUCTION

BODY

CONCLUSION

INSTRUCTOR'S COMMENTS

   Clarity of purpose . . . .

   Gesture-action-eye contact . . . .

   Language . . . .

   Voice . . . .

   Enthusiasm and vigor . . . .

   Self-confidence . . . .

   Organization . . . .

   Introduction and conclusion . . . .

   Grade . . . .

(List sources on back of page as indicated)

PRINTED SOURCES OF INFORMATION

Give complete information for each source.

1. Author's name . . . .
   Title of article. . . . .
   Book or magazine containing article . . . .
   . . . . Date of publication . . . .
   Chapters and/or pages containing material. . . . .

2. Author's name . . . .
   Title of article. . . . .
   Book or magazine containing article . . . .
   . . . . Date of publication . . . .
   Chapters and/or pages containing material . . . .

3. Author's name . . . .
   Title of article. . . . .
   Book or magazine containing article . . . .
   . . . . Date of publication . . . .
   Chapters and/or pages containing material. . . . .

INTERVIEW SOURCES OF INFORMATION

1. Name of person interviewed. . . . . Date of interview . . . .
   His title, position, and occupation . . . .
   . . . .
   Why is he an authority on the subject? Be specific. . . . .
   . . . .

2. Name of person interviewed. . . . . Date of interview . . . .
   His title, position, and occupation . . . .
   . . . .
   Why is he an authority on the subject? Be specific. . . . .
   . . . .

3. Name of person interviewed. . . . . Date of interview . . . .
   His title, position, and occupation . . . .
   . . . .
   Why is he an authority on the subject? Be specific. . . . .
   . . . .

PROJECT 25

THE DEDICATION SPEECH

You may not give a speech at dedication ceremonies for a long time, if ever; then again the occasion for a speech of this kind may arise sooner than you had thought possible. But regardless of when you are called on, you need to know its requirements. The dedication speech is given on an occasion and in an atmosphere that require strict observance of certain aspects of speech making.

Explanation of the Dedication Speech

The dedication speech is presented on commemorative occasions. It is generally brief and has a serious tone. It employs excellent language, and demands careful construction, fine wording, and polished delivery. Its purpose should be to commemorate, to honor an occasion, and to praise the spirit of endeavor and progress that the dedication symbolizes. The speech should thrill the audience with pride regarding their community, ideals, and progress. Occasions for the dedication speech usually involve a group enterprise. Common among them are such occasions as erecting monuments, completing buildings, stadiums, swimming pools, and baseball parks, or laying corner-stones or opening institutions. Lincoln's speech at the dedication of the Gettysburg Cemetery, the *Gettysburg Address*, is one of the finest speeches ever made.

Suggested Topics for Dedication Speeches

1. Laying a cornerstone for a new church.
2. A monument to a great international figure.
3. A monument as a historical marker.
4. Laying a cornerstone for a new Lodge building.
5. A new city hospital.
6. A new swimming pool.
7. A new city hall.
8. A new baseball park.
9. A new library.
10. A new college.
11. A monument to a national hero.
12. A monument to honor the war dead.
13. A monument to a local citizen.
14. A new city park.
15. Laying the cornerstone for a new auditorium.
16. A new high-school building.
17. A new courthouse.
18. A new stadium.
19. Laying the cornerstone for a new Student Union building.
20. Speaker's choice.

How to Choose a Topic

This will involve a bit of imagination on your part; however, choose an occasion that you wish were actually true, really taking place. Be sure you would be thrilled by it.

How to Prepare a Dedication Speech

First, know your purpose. You are to compliment the ideals and achievements which the dedicated structure symbolizes, thus setting it apart for a certain use or purpose.

These are the points to cover in your speech. Give a brief history of events leading up to the present. Mention the sacrifice, the work, the ideals, and the service that lie behind the project. Explain the future use or work, the influence or significance that will be associated with the structure being dedicated. Place the emphasis on what the object being dedicated stands for (ideals, progress, loyalty) rather than on the object itself.

Organize your speech very carefully. Pay particular attention to the introduction, the conclusion — yes, everything in your speech. It must have order. To organize the speech you must first outline it. The wording follows. Do this meticulously. Do not be grandiose or grandiloquent, but be understandable and simple in language. The speech is serious. Leave humor at home.

How to Present a Dedication Speech

The attitude of the speaker should be one of appropriate dignity. Emotion and dignity should be properly blended to fit the noble sentiments that will be present. The adequacy and poise of the speaker should be obvious from his appearance, his bearing, and his self-confidence.

Bodily action must be keyed to the tone of the speech. The environment of the occasion may permit much action or limit it severely. If a public address system is used, the speaker may not move from the microphone. He can and should utilize gestures.

Whether speaking with the aid of a microphone or not, the voice should be full and resonant and easily heard. If the crowd is large, a slower speaking rate should be used. Articulation must be careful, yet not so much so that it becomes ponderous and labored. Voice and action must be in tune, neither one overbalancing the other. The speaker must be animated, alive to his purpose, desirous of communicating, and capable of presenting a polished speech.

BIBLIOGRAPHY

Borchers & Wise, chap. 13.
Brigance, *Speech Comp.*, pp. 312-317.
Brigance, *Spoken Word*, chap. 7.

Crocker, *Pub. Spkg.*, chap. 22.
Monroe, *Prin. & Types*, chap. 23.
O'Neill, pp. 341-355.
O'Neill & Weaver, chap. 30.

Name . . . . Date . . . . Type of speech . . . .

Specific purpose of this speech . . . .

. . . . No. of sources required . . . . . .

Sentence outline: 75-100 words.   Time limit: 3-4 minutes.   Speaking notes: None.

TITLE

INTRODUCTION

BODY

CONCLUSION

INSTRUCTOR'S COMMENTS

Clarity of purpose. . . . .

Gesture-action-eye contact . . . .

Language . . . .

Voice. . . . .

Enthusiasm and vigor . . . .

Self-confidence . . . .

Organization . . . .

Introduction and conclusion . . . .

Grade. . . . .

(List sources on back of page as indicated)

PRINTED SOURCES OF INFORMATION

Give complete information for each source.

1. Author's name . . . .
   Title of article . . . .
   Book or magazine containing article . . . .
   . . . . Date of publication . . . .
   Chapters and/or pages containing material . . . .

2. Author's name . . . .
   Title of article . . . .
   Book or magazine containing article . . . .
   . . . . Date of publication . . . .
   Chapters and/or pages containing material . . . .

3. Author's name . . . .
   Title of article . . . .
   Book or magazine containing article . . . .
   . . . . Date of publication . . . .
   Chapters and/or pages containing material . . . .

INTERVIEW SOURCES OF INFORMATION

1. Name of person interviewed . . . . Date of interview . . . .
   His title, position, and occupation . . . .
   . . . .
   Why is he an authority on the subject? Be specific. . . . .
   . . . .

2. Name of person interviewed . . . . Date of interview . . . .
   His title, position, and occupation . . . .
   . . . .
   Why is he an authority on the subject? Be specific. . . . .
   . . . .

3. Name of person interviewed . . . . Date of interview . . . .
   His title, position, and occupation . . . .
   . . . .
   Why is he an authority on the subject? Be specific. . . . .
   . . . .

PROJECT 26

THE ANNIVERSARY SPEECH

Explanation of the Anniversary Speech

The anniversary speech is presented in commemoration of an event, a person, or occasion in the past. Its purpose is to recall and remember the past so that we may more adequately serve the present and courageously prepare for the future. It will weigh the past, observe the blessings of the present, and look to the future optimistically. Elements of loyalty and patriotism usually are present.

Because this talk is similar to the dedication speech, its requirements for the speaker do not vary noticeably from those for the dedication speech. The speaker should be fully acquainted with the history, the present anniversary, and future plans as they pertain to it. You might think of the anniversary as a birthday celebration and incorporate all the ideals and ideas associated with such a day.

Occasions for anniversary speeches arise whenever the passing of time is marked by a pause in which people lay aside their work long enough to note what has been accomplished. Independence Day, the landing of the Pilgrims, Armistice Day, Thanksgiving, Christmas, Labor Day, the birthday of a national, state, or local figure are all examples of such occasions. Observance of the progress during a certain number of years of a business firm, a school, a church, a city, state, nation, or any organization, may form the basis of an anniversary speech. During recent years, many state centennials have been observed with considerable formality.

Suggested Occasions for an Anniversary Speech

1. Your college is a half century old.
2. Air-mail service was established . . . . years ago.
3. The radio, telephone, sewing machine, etc., were invented . . . . years ago.
4. Radium was discovered . . . . years ago.
5. Today is Lincoln's birthday (or anyone's).
6. Your business is fifty years old.
7. Today is Labor Day.
8. The fire department has been active . . . . years.
9. Your church was established . . . . years ago.
10. Today is Army Day.
11. Today your state is 100 years old.
12. The first airplane flight was made . . . . years ago.
13. This bridge was built . . . . years ago.
14. Your business produces its millionth car, watch, washing machine.
15. The first atomic bomb was exploded . . . . years ago.
16. Today is Armistice Day.
17. Your lodge is twenty-five years old.
18. The navy has an anniversary.
19. Your city observes a birthday.
20. Speaker's choice.

How to Choose a Topic for an Anniversary Speech

If you have a particular loyalty or devotion construct your speech around it at an imaginary or real anniversary. Otherwise select one of the above suggestions in which you have an interest. *Be sure you are interested in the topic you select.*

How to Prepare an Anniversary Speech

Remember that your purpose is to commemorate. Keep this in mind constantly. Your thoughts must be organized to achieve this end.

The organization of your speech is important. Include whatever is appropriate of the following points: Tell why you are especially interested in this anniversary. Show historically that the people and their ideals are responsible for the celebration. Trace the development of these ideals. Anecdotes, stories, incidents, and humor are appropriate and impressive if properly used. The past should live vividly again for your audience. Turn next to the present; compare it with the past. Avoid references to or implications of partisan or class views. Speak broadly for all the people by showing a spirit of friendliness and good will. Direct your energies toward unity and interest for the common good. Speak confidently of the future. By virtue of a splendid past and a significant present, the future holds promises of greater things to be. Indicate that the cooperation of everyone in a determined effort for greater service to mankind is the goal all are seeking. Show the relationship of this anniversary to the welfare of the state and nation.

How to Present an Anniversary Speech

Speak sincerely. If you cannot and do not mean what you say, you should not be speaking. Your bodily actions, your voice, your entire organism should evince sincerity. There should be no display of either voice or action.

BIBLIOGRAPHY

Borchers & Wise, chap. 13.
Brigance, *Speech Comp.*, pp. 312-317.
Brigance, *Spoken Word*, Chap. 7.

Glasgow, pp. 167-171.
O'Neill, pp. 341-355.
O'Neill & Weaver, chap. 30.

SPEECH OUTLINE, PROJECT 26

Name .... Date .... Type of speech ....

Specific purpose of this speech ....

....No. of sources required ......

Sentence outline: 75-100 words.   Time limit: 5-6 minutes.   Speaking notes: Preferably none.

TITLE

INTRODUCTION

BODY

CONCLUSION

INSTRUCTOR'S COMMENTS

   Clarity of purpose...

   Gesture-action-eye contact..

   Language ....

   Voice..

   Enthusiasm and vigor ....

   Self-confidence...

   Organization ....

   Introduction and conclusion ....

   Grade........

(List sources on back of page as indicated)

PRINTED SOURCES OF INFORMATION

Give complete information for each source.

1. Author's name . . . .
   Title of article. . . . .
   Book or magazine containing article . . . .
   . . . . Date of publication . . . .
   Chapters and/or pages containing material. . . . .
2. Author's name . . . .
   Title of article. . . . .
   Book or magazine containing article . . . .
   . . . . Date of publication . . . .
   Chapters and/or pages containing material. . . . .
3. Author's name . . . .
   Title of article. . . . .
   Book or magazine containing article . . . .
   . . . . Date of publication . . . .
   Chapters and/or pages containing material. . . . .

INTERVIEW SOURCES OF INFORMATION

1. Name of person interviewed. Date of interview. . . . .
   His title, position, and occupation . . . .
   . . . .
   Why is he an authority on the subject? Be specific. . . . .
   . . . .
2. Name of person interviewed. Date of interview. . . . .
   His title, position, and occupation . . . .
   . . . .
   Why is he an authority on the subject? Be specific. . . . .
   . . . .
3. Name of person interviewed. Date of interview. . . . .
   His title, position, and occupation . . . .
   . . . .
   Why is he an authority on the subject? Be specific. . . . .
   . . . .

THE SPEECH TO GET ACTION – ANY KIND

In the field of public address a speaker often wants his audience to take some action as a result of his speech. Since people tend to resent being told outright to do this or that, the speaker has to approach his request for action in a more persuasive manner. Hence he must know how to organize his speech and on what to base his appeals to the audience so they will want to do what he suggests. This project not only tells you how to organize and present such a speech, but by having you complete the assignment it offers you an opportunity actually to make the speech.

Explanation of the Speech to Get Action

In the speech to get action the speaker tries to get his audience to perform a certain action, either immediately or later. *This speech stresses the action to be taken.*

The purpose of the speech to get action is to present ideas, suggestions, and arguments in such a way that the audience will believe so strongly what the speaker tells them that they will actually carry out his suggestions. To accomplish this the speaker presents information which convinces them by facts, logic, and emotion that they should do what he says. He stimulates and arouses them to a point that they feel they want to do something. He tells them what to do and he *stresses that this action should be taken.* He may point out what will happen if they do not do this and what will happen if they do. He will of course show that the audience stands to gain by doing what he suggests.

Naturally, arduous preparation must go into the speech to insure the mastery of general and detailed information which can be delivered with vigor and confidence. The speaker himself must be firmly convinced of what he is saying. There can be no sham or pretense. He must be sincere.

Occasions for the speech to get action are common. Among them are political rallies for a particular candidate or platform. In civic meetings people are urged to give money for worthy causes, to sign petitions. At labor conventions and meetings workers are urged to vote to strike. At religious gatherings men and women are told to cease iniquitous activities, to join the church, to tithe, etc. Salesmen insist that people purchase their products. Teachers lecture their students on the desirability of more study. Whenever someone asks people to do something, a speech to activate is delivered.

Suggested Topics for the Speech to Get Action

1. Write a letter home today.
2. Sign a petition.
3. Go to church next Sunday.
4. Quit putting your feet on the furniture in the school lounge.
5. Attend the next school athletic contest.
6. Attend the next school assembly.
7. Attend a special exhibit.
8. Write your Congressman relative to certain legislation.
9. Enlist in the armed forces.
10. Go out on strike or do not go out on strike.
11. Visit a dentist to have your teeth examined.
12. Contribute to the Community Chest.
13. Donate money to a family in which the father was recently killed.
14. Quit wearing slacks to class (girls).
15. Contribute for the construction of a new hospital.
16. Give one day's time to helping construct a new public swimming pool.
17. Hunters, buy red hats and jackets.
18. Skiers, install safety binders on your skis.
19. Car owners, have your car's steering mechanism checked at once.
20. Speaker's choice.

How to Choose a Topic

There are several points to consider in choosing a topic for a speech to get action.

First, is it likely that your listeners will be in a mood to take the action you have in mind? It would be imprudent to ask an audience to do their Christmas shopping within the next ten days if Christmas is three months away. It would be just as unwise to try to sell fur coats to an audience in a southern climate where no fur coats are needed.

Second, select a topic involving a request for action that can be carried out by your audience. If you try to sell an article or get a contribution that is beyond the financial means of your listeners, you will waste everyone's time. If you ask them to go some place they can't visit, to donate something they do not possess, or to act against their moral code, you are asking for failure insofar as your attempt to activate is concerned.

Third, select a topic in which the action you call for is something the audience is willing to do at your request. Your choice of topic should be governed by your analysis of what your audience's attitude is toward you. Don't ask them to oppose certain legislative action by writing their Congressmen if they are all staunch Republicans and you are known to be a staunch Democrat.

How to Prepare a Speech to Get Action

First, decide exactly what action you will ask your audience to take. This must be definite. It must not be a generalized or hazy idea about some vague action. Until you know absolutely and positively the specific action you want, you are not ready to begin preparing your speech because you won't know what you are preparing for. Thus a complete sentence statement of your specific purpose is required. Write it out so that you can have it before you throughout your entire preparation.

Having decided on the action you want from your audience, organize your speech as follows:

1. Tell generally and in some detail what is now happening in regard to the subject you are talking about. Give facts, examples, illustrations, and testimony to make your ideas clear, but don't spend too much time on this part of your speech.

2. Show how this is affecting the lives of your listeners. Show definitely that it is costing them money, damaging their community, retarding their personal advancement, endangering their lives or their children's lives, giving them a bad name, that it is unsanitary, detrimental to community progress, etc. (Use whatever appeals are necessary to make your audience see that they are affected personally. Be sure to give evidence to support these appeals. Make this point clear but do not overwork it.)

3. Show what can be done to correct or change the situation, and indicate the action necessary for your hearers to take. The action you suggest at this time and your arguments to show that it should be taken will make up the major portion of your speech.

    A. Show what and how your audience will benefit personally and/or as a group if they take the action you suggest. *Be specific in pointing out what they stand to gain from the action.* Show how beneficial and helpful it will be to them. Appeal to their desire for money and wealth, security, fame, social status, prestige, or recognition. It is at this point that they must be convinced. If they believe that they will actually receive all the benefits you mention, it's a pretty safe bet they'll follow your suggestions. It is not necessary to get unanimous action, but only enough to make your efforts worth while.

    B. Show how easy it will be for them to take the action.

    C. Show that they can afford it if it takes money or goods.

    D. Show that they can spare the time if it takes time.

    E. Tell them specifically when to do it. Give the date and the time.

    F. Tell them where to do it. Name the exact location and give directions about how to get there.

    G. Tell them what equipment will be needed (if any).

    H. Give the names and addresses of specific persons to be contacted. Tell them when to make the contacts — the hours those persons are available.

    I. If a petition is to be signed, have several copies together with pencils to be passed around.

    J. Tell how to perform the action if there is any question regarding it.

4. Reiterate briefly the "bad things" that will happen if they do not take the action you suggest, then contrast this by repeating the "good things" that will follow if they do as you say. Conclude with well-planned remarks stating your confidence that they will do the right thing.

How to Present the Speech to Get Action

In this speech, as in any speech, you will find it to your advantage to be both sincere and personally convinced of what you seek to have your audience do. Be confident, poised, at ease, alert, appropriately dressed, and friendly. Naturally your enthusiasm and vigor will be geared to the occasion, the audience, the environment, and your own style of speaking. Earnestness is desirable.

Your bodily actions and gestures must be adjusted to all the elements of the speaking situation. Older and better educated audiences do not want as much vigor and activity as do less enlightened and younger groups. Speak accordingly.

Your language should be clear, vivid, and easily understood. The words should be "picture words" which tell or describe your ideas so well that the audience immediately picture in their minds what you are talking about. Simple, descriptive language which brings up pictures, memories, images, and matters close to your listeners' way of living is most effective. There should be no display of vocabulary, no use of dollar words just for the sake of sounding big. The thing that counts most is language that says something which can be readily understood by those who hear you.

Say "we" when speaking to your audience. If you constantly refer to your listeners as "you," they may and usually do wonder what you yourself are going to do about the action you are asking them to take. By using "we" instead of "you" the audience immediately includes you as one of them.

On many occasions when action is sought from a group, certain persons in the audience agree beforehand to do what the speaker asks as soon as he asks for it. In this way they lead off and set the pace, thus inducing others to follow. Sometimes people are "planted" in the audience, or demonstrations are prearranged, to do certain things that will influence the audience — for example, the deafening fanfare, parading, beating of drums, and waving of signs at political conventions. All this is designed to get action of a very specific nature — vote for my candidate. Generally it is a significant part of the nominating speech in national conventions. The ethics and effectiveness of this type of activity may be open to question; however, the fact remains that it is done. Each speaker must decide for himself whether or not he wishes to use it as part of his presentation.

Other methods are used to influence the behavior of an audience so they will respond as desired. Thus charts and drawings, pictures, diagrams, and graphs may be exhibited. Sometimes group singing is used to get the audience in a receptive mood. Moving pictures are shown to demonstrate ideas and arguments. Printed matter is passed out to be read. It is usually unwise, however, to have anything distributed *during* your speech because it will draw the audience's attention away from what you are saying; furthermore, it creates a noisy disturbance. If material is to be distributed, do it before you start speaking or after you conclude. If it is done before, the audience can examine it and satisfy their curiosity, referring later to a specific portion which you ask them to read with you. If the material is distributed after you finish speaking, be prepared to answer questions about it or to discuss it if any questions arise.

BIBLIOGRAPHY

Baird & Knower, chap. 20.
Bryant & Wallace, *Fund.*, pp. 439-441.
Crocker, *Pub. Spkg.*, chap. 23.
Gray & Braden, chap. 3.
Huston & Sandberg, chap. 7.
Monroe, *Prin. & Types*, chap. 22.
Oliver & Cortright, chap. 16.
Oliver, Dickey & Zelko, pp. 221-259.
O'Neill, pp. 117-141.
Parrish, *Spkg. in Pub.*, pp. 344-382.
Sandford & Yeager, *Prin.*, 4th ed., pp. 157-175.
Sarett & Foster, chap. 19.
Thonssen & Scanlan, chap. 9.
Williamson & others, chap. 20.
Yeager, chap. 11.

SPEECH OUTLINE, PROJECT 27

Name . . . . Date . . . . Type of speech . . . .

Specific purpose of this speech . . . .

. . . . .No. of sources required . . . . . .

Sentence outline: 75-150 words.   Time limit: 5-6 minutes.   Speaking notes: 10 words.

TITLE

INTRODUCTION

BODY

CONCLUSION

INSTRUCTOR'S COMMENTS

Clarity of purpose . . . .

Gesture-action-eye contact . . . .

Language . . . .

Voice . . . .

Enthusiasm and vigor . . . .

Self-confidence . . . .

Organization . . . .

Introduction and conclusion . . . .

Grade . . . .

(List sources on back of page as indicated)

PRINTED SOURCES OF INFORMATION

Give complete information for each source.

1. Author's name . . . .

    Title of article . . . .

    Book or magazine containing article . . . .

    . . . . Date of publication . . . .

    Chapters and/or pages containing material . . . .

2. Author's name . . . .

    Title of article . . . .

    Book or magazine containing article . . . .

    . . . . Date of publication . . . .

    Chapters and/or pages containing material . . . .

3. Author's name . . . .

    Title of article . . . .

    Book or magazine containing article . . . .

    . . . . Date of publication . . . .

    Chapters and/or pages containing material . . . .

INTERVIEW SOURCES OF INFORMATION

1. Name of person interviewed . . . . Date of interview . . . .

    His title, position, and occupation . . . .

    . . . .

    Why is he an authority on the subject? Be specific. . . . .

    . . . .

2. Name of person interviewed . . . . Date of interview . . . .

    His title, position, and occupation . . . .

    . . . .

    Why is he an authority on the subject? Be specific. . . . .

    . . . .

3. Name of person interviewed . . . . Date of interview . . . .

    His title, position, and occupation . . . .

    . . . .

    Why is he an authority on the subject? Be specific. . . . .

    . . . .

THE NOMINATING SPEECH

How many times have you heard the remark, "I wish I had nominated George Potter for president last night; I almost did. He's a lot better man than John Dalton." But the sad fact remains that George Potter, well qualified and capable, was not nominated. Why? Probably because the person who wanted to nominate him lacked the courage to get on his feet and also lacked the knowledge of what to say in order to nominate him effectively. It is to be hoped that if you ever wish to nominate a capable leader, you will have the courage to rise and speak and the knowledge to utter appropriate thoughts.

Explanation of the Nominating Speech

A nominating speech is one in which a speaker places the name of another person before an assembly as a candidate for office. The speech is usually not long, often lasting only a few minutes. In presenting the candidate to the audience, the speaker tells why his man is especially fitted for the office in question. All remarks made by the nominator should be expressed in such a way that they set forth, in an orderly manner, the reasons why the candidate should be elected.

Before a speaker can make a nomination, the chairman of the assembly must announce that nominations for the . . . . . office are in order. The speaker must be recognized by the chairman. This is accomplished when the speaker rises and addresses the chair by saying, "Mr. Chairman," the presiding officer then giving the speaker permission to speak either by calling his name, by nodding, or by using some other word or sign. Only then is the nominating speech in order.

Common occasions for nominating speeches occur at meetings of political delegates, church bodies, fraternity and sorority members, civic organizations, councils, charitable groups, businessmen, labor unions, school people, and other similar groups.

Suggested Nominating Speeches

Nominate a candidate for one of the following positions:
1. Candidate for "good citizenship award."
2. Candidate for "safety award."
3. Most valuable athlete.
4. President of any civic organization.
5. Representative.
6. Mayor.
7. Prom chairman.
8. Candidate for "outstanding student" award.
9. Student council president.
10. Captain of a team.
11. Candidate for "good driving award."
12. Boy Scout leader.
13. Officer of the student legislature.
14. Senator.
15. City council.
16. Governor.
17. "Most popular student."
18. All-school representative.
19. Class officer.
20. Speaker's choice.

How to Choose a Candidate for a Nominating Speech

First, have confidence in the ability of the person you nominate. Second, be sure that he will be acceptable as a candidate. Choose someone reasonably well known, with a good record. Make certain that if he is elected he will do his work creditably.

How to Prepare the Nominating Speech

The purpose of this speech is to establish your candidate as the one best suited for the position to be filled. It is obvious that all the elements of the speech should point in one direction: Elect This Candidate! A careful organization should be worked out in which the arrangement is somewhat as follows: Name the office, set forth its specific requirements, and indicate what its needs are. Once these points are established, show that your candidate has exceptional fitness to satisfy all the needs and demands of the office. *Be specific.* Mention his training, experience, abilities (especially leadership and cooperation with people), and outstanding qualities of personality and character; clinch your argument with a statement to the effect that he is undoubtedly the person best fitted for the office. If your candidate is well known, you may present his name at the conclusion of your speech. If he is not well known, it is advisable to offer his name earlier, mention it again once or twice at appropriate points, and conclude with it.

How to Present the Nominating Speech

Have confidence in yourself and in your candidate. The audience can and will sense this. The speaker may achieve the appearance of self-confidence by an alert posture. The use of appropriate bodily action and gesture gives evidence of poise and confidence. The words of the speech must be vivid, descriptive, and meaningful. There must be a fluency and readiness of speech that fairly shout to your auditors that you *know* what you are talking about and that you want them to understand how important it is for the right man (your man) to be elected to office. Your emphasis, spontaneity, and sincerity must be manifested by your entire organism. This will be shown by what you do, the way you look, and how you sound. Avoid giving the appearance of being overconfident, overbearing, or conceited. Have a lively, energetic, unhesitant manner, as well as a pleasant, confident voice, an appropriate appearance, and a sincere desire to communicate.

BIBLIOGRAPHY

Borchers & Wise, chap. 13.
Brigance, *Speech Comp.*, pp. 312-323.
Brigance, *Spoken Word*, chap. 7.
Crocker, *Pub. Spkg.*, chap. 22.

Glasgow, pp. 165-166
Monroe, *Prin. & Types*, chap. 23.
O'Neill & Weaver, chap. 30.
Woolbert & Weaver, chap. 5.

SPEECH OUTLINE, PROJECT 28

Name . . . . Date . . . . .Type of speech . . . .

Specific purpose of this speech . . . .

. . . . .No. of sources required . . . . . .

Sentence outline: 75-100 words.   Time limit: 2-4 minutes.   Speaking notes: None.

TITLE

INTRODUCTION

BODY

CONCLUSION

INSTRUCTOR'S COMMENTS

   Clarity of purpose . . . .

   Gesture-action-eye contact . . . .

   Language . . . .

   Voice . . . .

   Enthusiasm and vigor . . . .

   Self-confidence . . . .

   Organization . . . .

   Introduction and conclusion . . . .

   Grade . . . .

(List sources on back of page as indicated)

PRINTED SOURCES OF INFORMATION

Give complete information for each source.

1. Author's name . . . .
   Title of article. . . . .
   Book or magazine containing article . . . .
   . . . . Date of publication . . . .
   Chapters and/or pages containing material . . . .

2. Author's name . . . .
   Title of article. . . . .
   Book or magazine containing article . . . .
   . . . . Date of publication . . . .
   Chapters and/or pages containing material . . . .

3. Author's name . . . .
   Title of article. . . . .
   Book or magazine containing article . . . .
   . . . . Date of publication . . . .
   Chapters and/or pages containing material . . . .

INTERVIEW SOURCES OF INFORMATION

1. Name of person interviewed. . . . . Date of interview . . . .
   His title, position, and occupation . . . .
   . . . .
   Why is he an authority on the subject? Be specific . . . .
   . . . .

2. Name of person interviewed. . . . . Date of interview . . . .
   His title, position, and occupation . . . .
   . . . .
   Why is he an authority on the subject? Be specific . . . .
   . . . .

3. Name of person interviewed. . . . . Date of interview . . . .
   His title, position, and occupation . . . .
   . . . .
   Why is he an authority on the subject? Be specific . . . .
   . . . .

PROJECT 29

THE SPEECH TO ACCEPT A NOMINATION OR OFFICE

Though right now you may think yourself the last person in the world who will ever be nominated for an office or elected to one, you may nevertheless someday be asked to perform public service; you may even seek nomination for public office.

Explanation of the Speech to Accept a Nomination or Office

This speech is one in which you publicly accept your own nomination or election to an office. The speech is much the same for either occasion.

Your speech should firmly establish you as a person of ability, courage, and modesty. It should create confidence in you in the minds of the audience. Your purpose is to establish this confidence. An occasion of this sort is potentially important. Since anything you say may be used for or against you, it is essential to say the right thing.

Occasions for speeches accepting a nomination or office may arise any time that candidates are selected or elections held. The selection of officers for private clubs, social and civic organizations, schools, churches, fraternal groups, and other similar bodies offers occasion for the acceptance speech. In most instances, however, candidates do not make a speech when nominated; such a speech is usually made only on election.

Suggestions for the Speech to Accept a Nomination or Office

Accept nomination or election for one of the following:
1. Official of a sportsman's club.
2. Official of a charitable society.
3. Official of a corporation.
4. Official of a veterans organization.
5. Official of a bank.
6. Official of a religious organization.
7. Official of a service organization.
8. Student body president.
9. Class president.
10. Official of a taxpayers league.
11. Official of a professional organization.
12. Official of a Chamber of Commerce.
13. Official such as a health organization executive.
14. Official of a state government.
15. Official of the national park system.
16. Official of a farm organization.
17. Official of a fraternity or sorority.
18. Student council president.
19. Official of a country club.
20. Speaker's choice.

How to Prepare a Speech to Accept a Nomination or Office

Consider the purpose of your speech—to establish yourself as a leader and to impress on people your capability as a leader so that they will vote for you for office. To accomplish this, you generally speak somewhat as follows: In appropriate and well-chosen words express your appreciation and thanks for the honor conferred upon you. (Do not talk *about* yourself.) Speak about the organization and its importance. Commend its history, its achievements, and its principles. Explain how these have made it grow and how they will continue in the future. You may pay tribute to famous great men of the past in the organization. Promise to uphold their ideals. Pledge your loyalty and support to the principles of the organization. Say frankly that you accept the nomination or office with complete realization of its responsibilities and that you intend to

(115)

carry them out. It is appropriate as your final remark to express again your appreciation of the honor conferred upon you.

A few points to keep in mind: Do not belittle yourself or express doubt regarding your fitness. Do not express surprise at your nomination or election; this was worn out long ago, and there is little truth or sincerity in it anyhow. In no way should you "let the people down" by causing them to feel that they have made a mistake. Use simple and sincere language.

How to Present a Speech to Accept a Nomination or Office

Your attitude should be one of dignity, friendliness, sincerity, and enthusiasm. Your manner, your voice, your bodily actions and gestures should all reflect your attitude. Be sure your dress is appropriate to the occasion, the audience, and yourself.

If there is applause when you rise to speak, wait until it subsides before you begin. If it continues, raise your hand to ask for silence and a chance to speak. Talk loudly enough to be heard by all, speak clearly and distinctly, and do not talk either too fast or too slowly. If your voice echoes, slow down.

BIBLIOGRAPHY

Baker, chap. 13.   Brigance, *Spoken Word*, chap. 7.   O'Neill & Weaver, chap. 26.

SPEECH OUTLINE, PROJECT 29

Name . . . . Date . . . . .Type of speech . . . .

Specific purpose of this speech . . . .

. . . . .No. of sources required . . . . . .

Sentence outline: 50-75 words.　　Time limit: 1-3 minutes.　　Speaking notes: None.

TITLE

INTRODUCTION

BODY

CONCLUSION

INSTRUCTOR'S COMMENTS

Clarity of purpose. . . . .

Gesture-action-eye contact . . . .

Language . . . .

Voice. . . . .

Enthusiasm and vigor. . . . .

Self-confidence . . . .

Organization . . . .

Introduction and conclusion . . . .

Grade. . . . .

(List sources on back of page as indicated)

PRINTED SOURCES OF INFORMATION

Give complete information for each source.

1. Author's name ....

   Title of article..

   Book or magazine containing article ....

   .... Date of publication...............

   Chapters and/or pages containing material......................................

2. Author's name ....

   Title of article..

   Book or magazine containing article ....

   .... Date of publication...............

   Chapters and/or pages containing material......................................

3. Author's name ....

   Title of article..

   Book or magazine containing article ....

   .... Date of publication...............

   Chapters and/or pages containing material......................................

INTERVIEW SOURCES OF INFORMATION

1. Name of person interviewed........................ Date of interview..........

   His title, position, and occupation ....

   ....

   Why is he an authority on the subject? Be specific ....

   ....

2. Name of person interviewed........................ Date of interview..........

   His title, position, and occupation ....

   ....

   Why is he an authority on the subject? Be specific ....

   ....

3. Name of person interviewed........................ Date of interview..........

   His title, position, and occupation ....

   ....

   Why is he an authority on the subject? Be specific ....

   ....

THE SALES TALK

The sales talk is something you may be called upon to present much sooner than you expect. It involves a situation in which you usually try to sell a group of persons an article in exchange for their money. Sometimes this is difficult. Many persons have had little or no experience in this particular type of speaking and selling. This one experience is not intended to make a sales expert of anyone, but certainly it will help the person who later finds it necessary to sell something to a group.

Explanation of the Sales Talk

In a sales talk you attempt to persuade a person or group to buy a product from you now or at a later date. In some instances you actually take orders at the conclusion of your remarks; in other cases you merely stimulate an interest in your goods so that prospective customers will buy from you later. But in either case, your purpose is to sell by stimulating the customer to want what you have for sale and to be willing to part with his money to acquire it.

The sales talk makes special demands on the speaker. He must be pleasing in appearance, pleasant to meet, congenial, and friendly. He must be thoroughly familiar with his product and with all matters pertaining to it, including many details. He should by all means be able and willing to answer questions regarding its production, the manufacturer (or the company sponsoring it, such as an insurance company), the cost, terms of sale, guarantees, repairs, cost of upkeep, and other such matters about his product. He should know how to meet objections, questions, or comparisons of it with competing products.

Occasions for the sales talk are many; any time a speaker appears before one or more persons for the purpose of selling, he makes a sales talk. The people who compose the audience may be a school board, a high-school or college class, church officials, a purchasing committee for a business house, a city council, a ladies' aid society, or a group of farmers who have met at a country schoolhouse to see a demonstration of a new tractor hitch. Prospective customers can be any kind of people and be met anywhere and at any time.

Suggested Topics for a Sales Talk

Build your speech around an attempt to sell one of the following:
1. Tickets to a movie, a play, sports contest, etc.
2. Clothing (any article).
3. Real estate or other property, oil stock, mining stock.
4. An insurance policy, any kind.
5. A watch, new or old.
6. A pen or pencil.
7. A vacuum cleaner.
8. Plows, drills, etc.
9. Fishing equipment, all kinds.
10. Sporting equipment — skis, golf clubs, tennis rackets, etc.
11. Old coins or stamps.
12. Commercial time on a radio station.
13. Kitchen equipment.
14. Food.
15. Stationery.
16. An electric razor.
17. Books or magazines.
18. A tractor, car, truck.
19. Hunting equipment — guns, ammunition, clothing, etc.
20. Speaker's choice.

How to choose a Topic for a Sales Talk

Choose a product that *you believe in;* then build your talk around it. Be sure to select something your audience can use. If none of the above suggestions is suitable, select something else.

How to Prepare a Sales Talk

Follow the regular steps of preparation for any speech. Pay particular attention to analyzing your audience. It would be fatal to misjudge your prospective buyers. You should know as much as possible about such items as the following: their probable income, credit rating, occupation, religion, education, local beliefs. A wise salesman will find out what other salesmen have sold or tried to sell this group in the way of competing products. He will also be familiar enough with these products so he can make comparisons favorable to his own product.

It is advisable, if possible, to demonstrate whatever you are selling. This means that you must know how to show it to the best advantage. Be sure that it makes a good appearance and is in good working order. Let your customers try it out.

Be ready to take orders. This will necessitate having pen and ink, order forms, credit information, checkbooks, and receipts. Do not make a buyer wait when he is ready to buy.

Be prepared to greet the audience promptly. Go to the designated meeting place early. Have everything properly and neatly arranged before your audience arrives. After you think you have every display most advantageously placed, all the sales forms in order, and everything else in tiptop shape, go back for a final check.

As for your speech, have it thoroughly in mind. Do not use notes. Obviously it is foolish to try to sell anything if you have to consult notes in order to remember its good points.

The organization of your speech should be well thought out. Here is a possible plan.

Have a friendly introduction; state your pleasure in meeting the audience. Be sincere.

Present information about yourself and your product. Who are you? What position do you hold? How long have you been with this company? Why did you choose to work for it? What is the name of the company? How old is it? Is it a nation-wide organization? Is it financially sound? Is it reliable? Does it stand behind its products? Does it guarantee its products? Does it quibble over an adjustment if a customer asks for one? Does it have a large dealer organization? Can you get parts and repairs quickly if these are needed? Does the company plan to stay in business? Is it constantly improving its products? Does it test all its products before placing them on the market? How large is its business? What special recommendations does it have? It may not be necessary to answer all these questions; however, many of them will be asked. In answering them, give information which establishes you as a reputable salesman and your company as a reputable firm.

Now that you have laid the groundwork, you are ready to show and explain the goods you have for sale. The nature of the article you are selling will determine how you do this. Probably the first thing you will do will be to explain the purpose of your product. Then explain and demonstrate how it operates. In doing this, be sure to play up its advantages, special features, new improvements, economy of operation, dependability, beauty, ease of handling, and the like. Give enough detail to be clear but not so much that you confuse your listeners.

At this point you have established yourself and your company, and you have explained and demonstrated your product. Your next step — *showing how your product will benefit its purchasers* — requires careful analysis of your audience. You must know their wants and needs and show them vividly *how your product satisfies these wants and needs.* If the article is a tractor, a farmer will do his work more easily and economically by using it. If it is a correspondence course, the buyer will make more money, gain prestige, secure advancement from the course. Whatever the item, show the advantages and benefits of owning it. Sometimes it is helpful to mention the names of other persons who have bought the product from you and are now enjoying owning it.

And now comes the last step. How can they buy it? Where? When? Who stocks it, if you carry only samples? How much does it cost? Do you sell on the installment plan? What are the carrying charges? How much do you require as a down payment? How many months are allowed to pay for it? What is the monthly payment? Or is it sold only for cash? Is any discount allowed for cash?

What special inducement is offered to those who buy now? How much can they save? Will future prices be higher? Do you take trade-ins? How much allowance is made on a trade-in? Make it as easy and simple as possible to buy the goods you are selling. Be sure that your explanations are clear and exact. Do not use misleading terms or give wrong impressions. If your salesmanship will not stand a full, complete, and candid examination, you will be wise to change your policies or your vocation.

Be sure to rehearse the demonstration and accompanying speech aloud many times, until you have attained complete mastery of the entire speech. Avoid being trite, cocky, or insincere.

How to Present a Sales Talk

Look good; be good. In other words, have a neat and pleasing appearance, plus a friendly and polite attitude. These points are extremely important. Your own good judgment will tell you what dress is appropriate. Your common sense will provide the background for the right attitude. Generally, begin your speech directly, if this is appropriate to the mood of your listeners. Avoid being smart or using questionable stories to impress them. Put the group at ease and get on with your speech. Your manner should be conversational, your voice easily heard by all but not strained. Your bodily action should be suitable for holding attention, making transitions, and demonstrating what you are selling. Your language, of course, should be simple, descriptive, vivid, and devoid of technical terms. In using charts, pictures, diagrams, or the article itself, your familiarity with them should be so great that you can point out any part of the product while retaining a position that permits focusing your attention on the audience. In answering questions be as clear as possible and be sure that your questioner is satisfied with the information you give. An alert and enthusiastic yet friendly attitude is most desirable.

Special Hints. Do not knock your competitor or his product; it is better to praise them. If you offer any special inducements to encourage the buying of your product, be sure to present them at the appropriate time. After concluding your talk, allow your audience time to ask questions. Some may want to ask questions during your speech. In this case, be sure to answer them clearly; however, do not turn the meeting into a question-and-answer session before describing your wares.

BIBLIOGRAPHY

Baker, chap. 20.
Brigance, *Speech Comp.*, pp. 292-293.
Buehler, part 2, chap. 4.
Goode, chaps. 6, 7.
Hibbitt, chap. 13.
Hickerson, complete book.

Ivey, complete book.
Printers Ink, chaps. 6, 7, 9, 10.
Roth, complete book.
Russell & Beach, complete book.
Sutton, complete book.
Thonssen & Scanlan, chap. 9.
Whiting, complete book.

SPEECH OUTLINE, PROJECT 30

Name . . . . Date . . . . Type of speech . . . .

Specific purpose of this speech . . . .

. . . . No. of sources required . . . . . .

Sentence outline: 75-100 words.   Speaking notes: None.

Time limit: 4-5 minutes followed by 3-minute period for questions from audience.

TITLE

INTRODUCTION

BODY

CONCLUSION

INSTRUCTOR'S COMMENTS

Clarity of purpose . . . .

Gesture-action-eye contact . . . .

Language . . . .

Voice . . . .

Enthusiasm and vigor . . . .

Self-confidence . . . .

Organization . . . .

Introduction and conclusion . . . .

Grade . . . .

(List sources on back of page as indicated)

PRINTED SOURCES OF INFORMATION

Give complete information for each source.

1. Author's name . . . .
   Title of article. . . . .
   Book or magazine containing article . . . .
   . . . . Date of publication . . . .
   Chapters and/or pages containing material . . . .

2. Author's name . . . .
   Title of article. . . . .
   Book or magazine containing article . . . .
   . . . . Date of publication . . . .
   Chapters and/or pages containing material . . . .

3. Author's name . . . .
   Title of article. . . . .
   Book or magazine containing article . . . .
   . . . . Date of publication . . . .
   Chapters and/or pages containing material . . . .

INTERVIEW SOURCES OF INFORMATION

1. Name of person interviewed. . . . . Date of interview . . . .
   His title, position, and occupation . . . .
   . . . .
   Why is he an authority on the subject? Be specific. . . . .
   . . . .

2. Name of person interviewed. . . . . Date of interview . . . .
   His title, position, and occupation . . . .
   . . . .
   Why is he an authority on the subject? Be specific. . . . .
   . . . .

3. Name of person interviewed. . . . . Date of interview . . . .
   His title, position, and occupation . . . .
   . . . .
   Why is he an authority on the subject? Be specific. . . . .
   . . . .

THE HUMOROUS SPEECH

There is a common misconception about the difficulty of giving a speech to entertain. The idea is current that such a speech is a "breeze," that nothing is difficult about it, that a series of risque stories meets the requirements for it. This is far from the truth; a humorous speech is one of the most difficult to present effectively.

Explanation of the Humorous Speech

A humorous speech may rely on words, anecdotes, bodily actions, gestures, voice, speech construction, special devices, demonstrations, unusual situations, pantomimes, or a combination of any or all of these factors.

Its purpose varies in relation to both the amount and the type of humorous response desired from the audience. Some speeches make their hearers laugh gaily and loudly; others produce only chuckles and snickers; still others bring forth only grins and smiles of amusement. A humorous speech does not need to be uproariously funny to entertain.

The special feature of a humorous speech is that it demands only that a speaker catch the attention and interest of an audience and then hold these by developing a trend of thought or an idea. However, a humorous speech *may* do more than simply entertain. There is nothing to prevent its being informative, stimulating, or convincing, provided none of these goals becomes the chief aim of the speaker. *The chief aim of the speech is to entertain.* An idea may and usually should be the main road the speech travels. The humor is achieved by hitting a few bumps, skidding around a bit, getting stuck in a mud hole, having a flat tire, and flirting with the farmer's daughter, all the time keeping to the main highway. Thus when you arrive at your destination, you have traveled a straight road but you've had a pleasant time doing it.

The thought or ideas are the core of the speech around which humor is build. The overall effect is one in which the audience finds a definite trend of thought and philosophy presented delightfully and entertainingly.

Occasions for humorous speeches ordinarily arise at dinners, club meetings, special assemblies, parties, and other gatherings at which weighty discussions are inappropriate and out of harmony with the mood of the occasion.

Suggested Topics for a Humorous Speech

1. How to be a howling success.
2. How to be popular in college.
3. My great embarrassment.
4. Night life in a dormitory.
5. Get rich slowly—it's safer.
6. Pockets and my money.
7. Styles—the national handicap.
8. How to tell a joke.
9. Never say "yes" in the Army.
10. Shopping, the weekly hazard.
11. Bringing up father at our house.
12. How to get what you want—without paying.
13. Gold is where you find it if you dig.
14. I don't want to be married.
15. Go west, young man.
16. Woman's weakness is her most powerful weapon.
17. Men are not egotists.
18. Doodling.
19. Grandpa's first car.
20. Speaker's choice.

How to Choose a Topic for a Humorous Speech

In selecting a topic for a humorous speech, keep in mind the five necessary considerations that govern the selection of any speech topic, that is, the audience, the occasion, the speaker (you), the speech itself, and the surroundings in which it will be given. Your choice of a topic must be keyed to these controlling factors. You may have a mixed audience with widespread interests or tastes. You must consider the probable speaking environment. Of course, since you will be the speaker, the subject you choose must be one which you can present acceptably. The topic should be viewed from the standpoint of the time allowed for preparation, the availability of materials from which to build the speech, your own personality, your position in the community, your ability to present certain kinds of material and ideas, and your type of presentation. Choose your topic with all these considerations in mind.

How to Prepare a Humorous Speech

As in the preparation of any good speech, particular attention must be paid to the organization of points, arrangement of materials, and rehearsal. The purpose, to entertain, should be kept clearly in mind; the purpose is assisted by a thorough understanding of the methods to be used for fulfilling this purpose. This type of speech requires a considerable study of references and some consultation with your instructor. In addition to the factors of good speech preparation previously studied, ample rehearsal is essential. It is difficult to imagine anything more grotesque than a speaker who attempts to present a humorous speech but must constantly refer to notes because of inadequate preparation.

The humorous speech should not degenerate into a series of unrelated funny stories, nor should it consist merely of one story. Exaggerations or episodes used as illustrations must be related to the theme of the speech or in some way assist the speaker in making his point. Only careful preparation and rehearsal will assure a speaker that he is using his illustrations properly.

Among the devices sometimes used to achieve humor are the following:
1. Telling a joke on oneself.
2. Telling a joke on someone in the group or on some well-known person.
3. Making humorous reference to the speech situation or to the local, state, or national situation.
4. Mentioning the occasion or other occasions.
5. Associating a speech with past incidents that have been amusing.
6. "Panning" members of the group or local, state, national, or world figures.
7. Exaggeration.
8. Deliberate understatement.
9. Sudden change of thought.
10. Surprise thoughts.
11. Afterthoughts tacked on to the end of an otherwise serious statement.
12. Twisting ideas (do not overdo this).
13. Misinterpreting facts or figures (be clever about this).
14. Intentionally making errors (this must be skillfully done).
15. Intentionally placing oneself in a humorous situation.
16. Misquoting someone present or a well-known authority (be discreet).
17. Restating a well-known quotation to give it a humorous twist.
18. Pantomime (also humorous props or humorous use of props).
19. Gestures poorly timed or timed too late.
20. Facial grimaces.
21. Anecdotes.
22. Examples that are humorous or make an amusing point.
23. Impersonating a character used as an illustration (do not make your whole speech an impersonation).
24. Demonstrating or dramatizing a point (do this for purposes of illustrating to achieve humor).
25. Clever wording (concoct new words, apply certain words to new situations or give them new meanings, join two or more words together with hyphens, then apply them in your speech).

Be quick to adapt your opening remarks to slips of the tongue made by the toastmaster or other speakers. Do not overwork this device or it will become tiresome and trite; be appropriate.

Persons in public life, international situations, recent happenings in the news all offer excellent opportunities for humor.

A mechanical method for a humorous speech is to make a point and then tell two or three humorous stories or anecdotes to illustrate it. Repeat this procedure for several major points and you will have a humorous speech. All the major points and jokes should be connected by suitable transitions.

A speaker who selects a subject of serious or light nature and then humorously classifies people and/or events that come under it usually elicits excellent humorous responses.

By discussing a subject pro and con and using humorous arguments to establish both views humor is readily achieved.

Treating a light subject seriously can be humorous if it is cleverly done.

In actually setting up the humorous speech, follow the principles laid down for any speech. Construct a clever and interesting introduction; develop your remarks point by point in logical order; bolster these points with examples, illustrations, facts, quotations from authorities, analogies, and conclusions drawn from the material you present. Have a conclusion that is appropriate to all you have said. Thus it becomes evident that a speech to entertain does what every other speech does, and in addition—this is important—utilizes materials that in themselves carry and imply humor. The selection of these humorous materials, their arrangement in the speech, the words and the physical activity used to present them are what achieve the effect of entertainment.

You may ask, "How do I know my speech will be entertaining?" You don't. The only assurance you can have is from your preparation. Frankly this depends entirely on your own effort and ability. It is difficult to select, organize, word, and rehearse a speech to entertain, but you must do all these things nevertheless. Your own ingenuity and your own intelligence are the only assets you have in preparing a humorous speech. Use these inherent personal resources well and you will have little to worry about. There is no quick, easy way to prepare an entertaining speech—or any other kind, for that matter.

How to Present a Humorous Speech

The humorous speech is characterized generally by lively presentation. The speaker may be whimsical, facetious, gay, or jovial, or he may embody a mixture of these moods. He should be pleasant, of course. His entire bearing and decorum should visibly reflect the feelings and tenor of his remarks.

The speech should progress with a smooth forward motion. Avoid delays and hesitations, except those employed for a special effect. If there is laughter, refrain from resuming until you can be heard. Usually this is at the moment just before the laughter stops. Never laugh at your own jokes or indicate that you know you are funny. However, enjoy your audience and yourself, and let this be obvious.

One of the greatest dangers for the inexperienced speaker is that he will prolong his anecdotes, his jokes, or his whole speech. This may happen either because he is enjoying himself so much that he forgets to keep moving or because he has not properly prepared his speech. Then, too, nervousness may cause memory lapses and confusion. Strive to hit the punch lines when they are hot and then move on to the next ones.

BIBLIOGRAPHY

Brigance, *Speech Comm.*, pp. 117-118.
Brigance & Immel, chap. 13.
Bryant & Wallace, *Fund.*, pp. 560-563.
Buehler, part 2, chap. 4.
Butler, chap. 5.

Crocker, *Pub. Spkg.*, chap. 18.
Dolman, chap. 10.
Hibbitt, chaps. 23-30.
Monroe, *Prin. & Types*, chap. 15.
Norvelle & Smith, chap. 3.

Name .... Date ...... Type of speech ....

Specific purpose of this speech ....

.... No. of sources required ....

Sentence outline: 75-150 words. Time limit: 5-6 minutes. Speaking notes: None.

TITLE

INTRODUCTION

BODY

CONCLUSION

INSTRUCTOR'S COMMENTS

Clarity of purpose...

Gesture-action-eye contact ....

Language ....

Voice..

Enthusiasm and vigor ....

Self-confidence ....

Organization ....

Introduction and conclusion ....

Grade........

(List sources on back of page as indicated)

PRINTED SOURCES OF INFORMATION

Give complete information for each source.

1. Author's name . . . .
   Title of article . . . .
   Book or magazine containing article . . . .
   . . . . Date of publication . . . .
   Chapters and/or pages containing material . . . .

2. Author's name . . . .
   Title of article . . . .
   Book or magazine containing article . . . .
   . . . . Date of publication . . . .
   Chapters and/or pages containing material . . . .

3. Author's name . . . .
   Title of article . . . .
   Book or magazine containing article . . . .
   . . . . Date of publication . . . .
   Chapters and/or pages containing material . . . .

INTERVIEW SOURCES OF INFORMATION

1. Name of person interviewed . . . . Date of interview . . . .
   His title, position, and occupation . . . .
   . . . .
   Why is he an authority on the subject? Be specific . . . .
   . . . .

2. Name of person interviewed . . . . Date of interview . . . .
   His title, position, and occupation . . . .
   . . . .
   Why is he an authority on the subject? Be specific . . . .
   . . . .

3. Name of person interviewed . . . . Date of interview . . . .
   His title, position, and occupation . . . .
   . . . .
   Why is he an authority on the subject? Be specific . . . .
   . . . .

AFTER-DINNER SPEAKING

One of the best ways to learn anything is to experience it. From the experience of preparing this speech assignment you will gain first-hand knowledge of after-dinner speaking. You will see how the program is arranged and how the toastmaster must keep it moving. You will acquire much other valuable information concerning after-dinner speaking. You will learn all this because you will help build the entire program and because you will be a speaker at the dinner.

If it is impossible to carry out a real banquet for this project, as many speech classes do, an alternative may be worked out in class. Have the students sit in a rectangular group to simulate positions around a table at a banquet. The toastmaster should be placed at the head of the imaginary table, with the speakers seated as they would be had the dinner just been completed. As far as possible, an after-dinner speech atmosphere and environment should be created. As another alternative to a real banquet, the students may eat lunch together in a suitable room somewhere in a college building. To make this experience completely real, the meeting should be held at a local hotel, cafe, or other place where the class can meet and eat without crowding. The atmosphere should be absolutely true to life, without make-believe, and guests should be invited.

Explanation of After-Dinner Speaking

The after-dinner speech may have a serious purpose or it may be designed solely to give entertainment and pleasure. Conventionally it usually calls for a light touch, a bit of gaiety, and a tone of optimism, all ingeniously woven into a pattern of originality. However, the type of speech you present depends on the purpose of your talk, the occasion, its objective, and the reason for your remarks. After-dinner speeches require that the speaker follow closely all the rules of organization previously noted, particularly those concerning serious talks. Humor as an objective necessitates altering the organization of the speech enough to make the ideas fulfill the purpose—entertaining humorously.

Occasions for the after-dinner speech are many—business luncheons, club dinners, committee meetings, special breakfasts, promotional gatherings, the launching of campaigns, celebrations, anniversaries, and dozens of other similar occasions.

Suggested Topics for After-Dinner Speeches

1. Bugs are my friends.
2. Money and women are easy to lose.
3. If I were king.
4. Gadgets—our greatest enemy.
5. Silence is not always golden.
6. Hard luck, my dilemma.
7. Gossip—a blessing in disguise.
8. My first job in the army.
9. The last days of a single man.
10. Fishermen—strange creatures.
11. Income taxes are too simple.
12. How to win friends and their money.
13. A successful man.
14. Of all sad words.
15. I wish I had not said it.
16. Why I read comics.
17. So you want to be a salesman.
18. Ten years from now.
19. If I had ten lives to live.
20. Speaker's choice.

Note: If a dinner is to have a particular theme, topics should be chosen that are in keeping with the theme.

How to Prepare an After-Dinner Speech

First of all, study this assignment carefully to learn all the requirements of successful after-dinner speaking. Follow previous instructions for speech organization, wording, and practice. Plan to speak without notes.

The speaker's obligations: The preparation of this talk is no different from that of any other speech, depending on the type you intend to present. If your thoughts are humorous, prepare a humorous speech; reread the preceding project on humorous speeches. Follow this procedure for any type of speech you wish to deliver, whether your purpose is to convince, to inform, or to stimulate.

Having decided on your subject and the way you will treat it, complete the preparation of your speech carefully. Before you consider yourself fully prepared, find out all you can about the program, when you will speak, and who will precede you. Then be sure that your speech is in line with the occasion.

It is not necessary and certainly not always advisable that a speaker plan to tell a joke on the toastmaster, regardless of what the toastmaster may do in the way of introduction. If the occasion calls for humor, be ready to meet it. If there is any doubt as to what to do, play it safe. Good taste never offends. As far as risque stories go, leave them at home. If you don't have a clean story that packs a wallop, you haven't tried to find one. The world has a great storehouse of humorous and clean stories for all who want them, and they are excellent for after-dinner speeches.

To complete the preparation of your after-dinner speech, practice it aloud several times before a mirror. It is a good idea to ask one or more friends to hear you in rehearsal. But before you take their advice or criticisms too literally, give some thought to their suggestions and the reliability of their advice.

The toastmaster's obligations: The toastmaster has an important task. He must see that everything is ready to go; he must open the proceedings, keep them going, and close the meeting. Let us examine these duties separately. First, to arrange everything, he should arrive at the meeting place early. He will then do the following chores: (1) If there is no dinner chairman, he will advise the waiters in detail as to how the meal is to be served. (2) He will note the arrangement of the banquet room and suggest any changes he desires. (3) He will indicate to the group when they are to go into the dining hall—that is, if they have been waiting in a lobby; if everyone has previously gathered in the dining room he will be the first to seek his chair as a signal that others should follow suit. (4) During the banquet he will be constantly alert to see that all goes well.

In regard to the actual work of introducing the speakers, considerable information must be gathered well in advance: (1) the names of the speakers; (2) their topics; (3) data concerning the speakers that are suitable to use when introducing them; (4) the order of the speakers. Introducing the speakers requires ingenuity and planning. A toastmaster should learn early that he is not to make speeches. This pleasure belongs to the after-dinner speakers. He merely presents each speaker by giving him a short introduction. Thirty seconds usually suffices, sometimes less, but never more than a minute or two. The introduction may be a clever statement or two about the speaker, his name, and his topic. A fitting anecdote is in order if the occasion demands it. After the speaker concludes his speech, the toastmaster should get on with the show and not devote any time to a rebuttal of something said by the speaker.

How to Present an After-Dinner Speech

Your presentation should reflect the type of speech you deliver. Generally, simple organization, graphic word pictures, sufficient humor, lively and animated delivery, and a forward movement of ideas characterize afer-dinner speeches.

Voice and bodily action should be in harmony with the occasion and the environment. The chances are that you will not need to talk loudly to be heard, nor will you be permitted much bodily action because of space limitations and arrangements. Take care when you rise to speak, lest your chair scrape noisily on the floor and make you appear awkward. To prevent this, see that it is far enough away from the table so that you can rise easily. When the chairman, toastmaster, or president introduces you, rise and address him according to his position—"Mr. Toastmaster," "Mr. Chairman," and the like. Keep your remarks in line with the occasion and purpose of your speech. "Ad-lib" and improvise as the situation demands. Retain a sense of humor, use it if it is appropriate, and observe your time limit. Remember that the program committee has allotted only a certain amount of time to you.

BIBLIOGRAPHY

Baker, chap. 17.
Borchers & Wise, chap. 13.
Borden, pp. 41-52.
Brigance, *Speech Comp.*, pp. 307-312.
Bryant & Wallace, *Fund.*, pp. 563-568.
Bryant & Wallace, *Oral Comm.*, chap. 13.
Buehler, part 2, chap. 4.
Butler, chap. 5.
Crocker, *Pub. Spkg.*, pp. 355-358.

Glasgow, pp. 176-184.
Hibbitt, chaps. 15, 16.
Meiers & Knapp, complete book.
Monroe, *Prin. & Types*, chap. 24.
Muller, complete book.
O'Neill, pp. 355-363.
Rango, complete book.
Woolbert & Weaver, chap. 5.

Name . . . . Date . . . . . . Type of speech . . . .

Specific purpose of this speech . . . .

. . . . No. of sources required . . . .

Time limit: 3 minutes.   Speaking notes: None.

Although you are not required to prepare an outline or to read source materials, it will be wise
to do both for your own benefit.

TITLE

INTRODUCTION

BODY

CONCLUSION

INSTRUCTOR'S COMMENTS

Clarity of purpose . . . .

Gesture-action-eye contact . . . .

Language . . . .

Voice . . . .

Enthusiasm and vigor . . . .

Self-confidence . . . .

Organization . . . .

Introduction and conclusion . . . .

Grade . . . .
                    (List sources on back of page as indicated)

(135)

PRINTED SOURCES OF INFORMATION

Give complete information for each source.

1. Author's name . . . .

   Title of article. . . . .

   Book or magazine containing article . . . .

   . . . . Date of publication . . . .

   Chapters and/or pages containing material. . . . .

2. Author's name . . . .

   Title of article. . . . .

   Book or magazine containing article . . . .

   . . . . Date of publication . . . .

   Chapters and/or pages containing material. . . . .

3. Author's name . . . .

   Title of article. . . . .

   Book or magazine containing article . . . .

   . . . . Date of publication . . . .

   Chapters and/or pages containing material. . . . .

INTERVIEW SOURCES OF INFORMATION

1. Name of person interviewed. . . . . Date of interview . . . .

   His title, position, and occupation . . . .

   . . . .

   Why is he an authority on the subject? Be specific. . . . .

   . . . .

2. Name of person interviewed. . . . . Date of interview . . . .

   His title, position, and occupation . . . .

   . . . .

   Why is he an authority on the subject? Be specific. . . . .

   . . . .

3. Name of person interviewed. . . . . Date of interview . . . .

   His title, position, and occupation . . . .

   . . . .

   Why is he an authority on the subject? Be specific. . . . .

   . . . .

IMPROMPTU SPEAKING

Time limit: 2, 3, 4, and 5 minutes. (Increase the length until students can talk five minutes.)

This speech experience exposes you to impromptu speaking and provides you with a rudimentary acquaintance with its nature and difficulties. Many students assume that impromptu speaking is easy. In reality it is extremely difficult. It is used effectively only by experienced speakers. There are, however, methods which, if properly used, will enable a person to perform acceptably on the spur of the moment.

Explanation of Impromptu Speaking

Impromptu speaking means giving an unprepared talk. A person simply selects a subject, goes to the rostrum, and begins. A speaker sometimes takes the floor after being asked to talk on a certain subject which he may or may not know much about. Or topics may be suggested by several persons in the audience; a few seconds are given the speaker to choose the one which he feels best suited to expound; then he begins. Differences in the manner of selecting a topic are many; however, a fundamental principle is that the ideas voiced about the topic are unprepared and unrehearsed.

The distinctive feature of impromptu speaking is the suddenness with which a person is confronted with a speech situation. One may be called upon without warning "to say a few words" at a luncheon, special meeting, social gathering, or other occasion.

Suggested Topics for Impromptu Speeches

In the space below, write three suggestions suitable for use as subjects. Avoid such topics as: "What Did You Do Last Night?" "A Trip to Yellowstone Park." Your instructor will ask you to supply a topic from time to time during the class. Suitable topics for impromptu speaking are: dancing; movies; trees; horses; strikes; liquor laws; divorce; narcotics; medicine; college athletics; current events; local politics.

1. ....
2. ....
3. ....

How to Prepare for an Impromptu Speech

Naturally you cannot prepare for an unknown topic, but you *can* prepare a method of attack on topics offered by your audience. One way of doing this is to have in mind various orders in which to develop your ideas.

One order might be a *time sequence* in which you discuss events in terms of the hour, day, month, or year, moving forward or backward from a certain time. A *space order* would take you from east to west, top to bottom, front to rear. Using *causal order*, you might discuss certain causes and then point out the results which follow. A *special order* is one of your own devising.

A most effective method is to narrow your subject, state its importance to the audience, present its history and development, discuss present conditions pro and con on a local, state, national, or world basis, predict future developments, and suggest what the audience should do in regard to it. Another method is to discuss the *past, present,* and *future* of the subject on political, economic social, religious, moral, and educational bases, or just discuss it in terms of the *past, present,* and *future.*

How to Present an Impromptu Speech

In presenting an impromptu speech your attitude is the deciding factor in determining your effectiveness. First of all, *maintain poise.* It is impossible to overemphasize the importance of poise. How do you maintain poise? Do not fidget in your seat before you speak, because you know you will soon be "on the spot." When you are called on, rise calmly and take your place before your audience. If you know your topic when you take the platform, begin your remarks calmly, without hurrying (have some vigor and force), and be sure that you have a plan in mind by which you will develop your thoughts. If you do not know your topic when you rise but are offered several choices after obtaining the floor, stand calmly before the group and listen carefully to the suggestions. Ask that a topic be repeated if you do not understand it. After you have heard all the proposed subjects, stand calmly or walk calmly back and forth a few seconds while you decide which one you will talk about. Once your selection is made, decide immediately what method you will use in developing it. As your introduction tell why the subject is important to your listeners. When you begin to speak, *do not make any apology whatsoever.* Get on with your speech.

In actually delivering an impromptu talk, it is wise not to start too fast but rather to pick up speed and power as you go along. Aside from this, observe bodily actions and gestures in keeping with the speech situation. Naturally, your articulation, pronunciation, and grammar should be of high standard.

There is little to fear from impromptu speaking if you follow a preconceived method of attack on your subject. Do not allow yourself to become panicky; remember that some nervousness is a good sign of readiness; and realize that your audience will expect nothing extraordinary from you because they too know you are speaking impromptu. Actually, they will be "pulling for you." If you go about your task with poise and determination, your chances of success are exceedingly good. A well-rounded knowledge attained from a consistent reading program will assist you immeasurably.

BIBLIOGRAPHY

Baker, chap. 18.
Bryant & Wallace, *Fund.*, pp. 314-321.
Butler, chap. 8.
Crocker, *Pub. Spkg.*, pp. 61-64.

Dolman, chap. 17.
Glasgow, pp. 158-160.
Hibbitt, chap. 17.
O'Neill, pp. 46-51.
Woolbert & Weaver, pp. 140-141.

PROJECT 34

THE BOOK REVIEW

Explanation of the Book Review

An oral book review is an orderly talk about a book and its author, including an evaluation of his work. The purpose of your talk is to inform, to stimulate, to entertain, and possibly to convince or get action.

The book reviewer is expected to know his material well, to be informed regarding the methods of giving a review, and to be able to present his information in an organized and interesting manner. These requirements demand unusually thorough preparation.

Occasions for the book review may arise almost anywhere. Reviews may be called for in scholarly, civic, religious, and other organizations. In practically any kind of club or society, school or church, a book review often is the basis of a program.

Suggested Types of Books for Review

For this particular experience it is suggested that each student select a different speech book to review, one approved by the instructor. If the instructor prefers, he may assign any type of book for review; however, reviews of speech books will provide a wide coverage of the field and a wealth of information in a short time.

How to Choose a Book for Review

If you are asked to review a speech text, go to the library, examine the tables of contents of several books carefully, and make your selection on the basis of their suitability, appeal, and interest to you and your audience. Do not choose a highly technical or scientific treatise on phonetics, rhetorical analysis, speech pathology, or a similar subject unless you have sufficient background to prepare a comprehensive and intelligible review. If you review an approved book that does not deal with speech, be sure that it is satisfactory for the occasion, the audience, and yourself.

How to Prepare a Book Review

Every speech must have a purpose, and the book review is no exception. For this reason, you first determine whether your purpose is to inform, to entertain, to convince, to stimulate, or to get action.

Next you ask, "What should go into a book review and how should I go about organizing my material?" The following suggestions may help you. Tell about the author. Who is he? What about his life? What anecdotes can you find about him? Does he do more than write? What other books has he written? Where does he live? What is his environment? How old is he? Include other data of a similar kind. Opinion varies regarding how much should be told about the author. Probably the criteria here are whether the book is fiction or nonfiction and who makes up the audience. Generally, though, be brief about the author.

Now, about the book. What is the title? Why did you choose it? Who is the publisher? When was it written? Under what circumstances? Why was it written? Is it biographical, historical, fiction, or what? What do the reviewers say about it? (Ask your librarian to show you book reviews such as those in the New York *Times, Christian Century, Saturday Review of Literature, New Republic, The Nation*, and others.) What is your opinion? Formulate your own; do not plagiarize someone else's evaluation of the book. Is the print clear and easily read? Is the format attractive?

For fiction, after you have presented background information about the author and the book, tell what the book is about. Mention the setting and the period in which it is laid. Describe the leading characters and important subordinate characters, telling briefly of their relationship and interplay in the story. Indicate the plot briefly by citing various incidents and events that reflect its development. Usually not much is disclosed concerning the outcome of the plot in order to stimulate reader interest. Some reviews, however, go into considerable detail for the express purpose of telling enough about the contents so that it is unnecessary for the listener to read the books.

When reviewing nonfiction and textbooks the reviewer usually gives the author's and book's background in more detail than in fiction. This assists in evaluating the book's validity. In nonfiction the reviewer attempts to ascertain what the author was trying to tell, how valid his material is, how well he develops his ideas, and the extent to which he was able to do what he set out to do. In covering these points the reviewer generally notes organization, use of illustration and example, consistency of ideas, and conclusions drawn. An evaluation is made of these.

In reviewing you may cite paragraphs or passages from the book as examples of what you are talking about. You should also refer to the contents as representing what the author thinks. Avoid a dull recitation of just the contents and also avoid presenting the contents as though they were your ideas. Evaluate the book as you present your review. This means discussing briefly the pro or con, the trite or unique, the doubtful or certain, the uselessness or usefulness, the practical or the impractical, among other points. Discuss these matters in relation to the material and state your point of view frequently as you proceed. Be sure to say whether or not you recommend the book and the restrictions or reservations with which you recommend it. Tell the audience where the book may be bought or rented.

One of the best ways to secure the above information is to read the book you are preparing to review several times. First, read it for enjoyment. The second and third times read for information you plan to use in your review. If time does not permit several readings, read it once carefully. As for getting your material in mind, use your own method. It is advisable either to write the speech out in full or to make a careful and detailed outline; then rehearse aloud until your sequence of thoughts is firmly fixed in your mind. If you use quotations, make them brief.

How to Present a Book Review

Have the review "in your head." Do not stand before your audience with the book in your hands so that you can use it as a crutch for referring to previously marked pages or for merely occupying the time by reading. This is not reviewing. Carry the book, yes, but use it for quotations. Have it with you to show the audience, if for no other reason. If you use notes, limit yourself to three words or less for each minute you speak.

BIBLIOGRAPHY

Book Review Digest.
Christian Century.
Crocker, Pub. Spkg., p. 366.

New Republic.
New York Times, book review sections.
Quarterly Journal of Speech, book review sections.
The Nation.

Name . . . . Date . . . . Type of speech . . . .

Specific purpose of this speech . . . .

. . . . No. of sources required . . . . . .

Sentence outline: 75-150 words.   Time limit: 15 minutes.   Speaking notes: 40-word limit.

TITLE

INTRODUCTION

BODY

CONCLUSION

INSTRUCTOR'S COMMENTS

Clarity of purpose . . . .

Gesture-action-eye contact . . . .

Language . . . .

Voice . . . .

Enthusiasm and vigor . . . .

Self-confidence . . . .

Organization . . . .

Introduction and conclusion . . . .

Grade . . . .

(List sources on back of page as indicated)

PRINTED SOURCES OF INFORMATION

Give complete information for each source.

1. Author's name . . . .

   Title of article. . . . .

   Book or magazine containing article . . . .

   . . . . Date of publication . . . .

   Chapters and/or pages containing material . . . .

2. Author's name . . . .

   Title of article. . . . .

   Book or magazine containing article . . . .

   . . . . Date of publication . . . .

   Chapters and/or pages containing material . . . .

3. Author's name . . . .

   Title of article. . . . .

   Book or magazine containing article . . . .

   . . . . Date of publication . . . .

   Chapters and/or pages containing material . . . .

INTERVIEW SOURCES OF INFORMATION

1. Name of person interviewed. . . . . Date of interview . . . .

   His title, position, and occupation . . . .

   . . . .

   Why is he an authority on the subject? Be specific . . . .

   . . . .

2. Name of person interviewed. . . . . Date of interview . . . .

   His title, position, and occupation . . . .

   . . . .

   Why is he an authority on the subject? Be specific . . . .

   . . . .

3. Name of person interviewed. . . . . Date of interview . . . .

   His title, position, and occupation . . . .

   . . . .

   Why is he an authority on the subject? Be specific . . . .

   . . . .

MANUSCRIPT SPEAKING

Manuscript speaking means reading a speech rather than presenting it extemporaneously, impromptu, or from memory. The only time it should be used is when a speaker has to state his ideas exactly to avoid being misquoted. Speakers in this category are high government officials and other individuals who dare not risk misunderstanding because of being misquoted.

Because of the very rigid time limits, station requirements, and the possible need for an exact copy for filing, practically all radio speeches are read.

Most people are not radio or television speakers, nor are they of great importance in the affairs of government. This means, then, that *most persons should not read manuscripts of speeches.* It isn't necessary, it isn't required, and usually it isn't well done. Do not read your speech except for radio or television, and perhaps not even then unless it seems particularly advisable.

If you do find it necessary to read a manuscript, there are several points to consider. First, in preparing your speech, write it so it will sound as though you were speaking extemporaneously. Make it conversational but at the same time observe all the attributes of effective word usage. Type it double-spaced.

Second, rehearse it enough so you can look at your audience most of the time. This requires a lot of practice and in the final analysis it demands that the manuscript be semi-memorized. Rehearsing before a mirror is an excellent way of gaining this proficiency.

Third, know the material so well that you won't mispronounce or stumble over any words or phrases. At the same time avoid developing vocal patterns or stereotyped reading habits that smack of reciting or reading. You must sound and appear as if you were talking extemporaneously. Some speakers depart momentarily from their script during reading, thus heightening the extempore effect; but this requires skill.

Fourth, handle your manuscript skillfully. Being awkward, shuffling the pages, losing your place, turning the pages clumsily, holding the script too close or too far away, peering at the words, or dropping pages can literally kill your speech.

Finally, observe the above points in conjunction with all the other elements of effective public speaking. These include desirable posture, effective facial, head, arm, and torso gestures, proper use of the voice, and a sincere desire to produce a specific response. Observance of these criteria will add much to your effectiveness when speaking from manuscript.

BIBLIOGRAPHY

Crocker, *Pub. Spkg.*, pp. 82-84.
Fessenden & Thompson, pp. 167-168.

Oliver & Cortright, pp. 543-547.
Soper, pp. 320-322.
Williamson & others, chaps. 21, 22.

PROJECT 36

RADIO SPEAKING

Time limit: To be assigned.

Speaking notes: Unless directed otherwise, you are to write out your speech word for word. A copy of it should be in your instructor's hand at least one day before you are scheduled to speak.

Sources of information: Two or more. List them at the end of your written speech.

Speech outline: None required for your instructor.

One who understands the preparation and presentation of radio speeches from first-hand knowledge and experience is much freer to evaluate and appreciate it, as well as participate in it. Real experience in studios provides at least an acquaintance with broadcasting and should enlighten and interest all speech students. It will pose real problems and answer many questions for all who take part.

In some cities the instructor will be able to arrange with a local broadcasting company for time at their studios. Two rooms should be used, one with a microphone from which to broadcast, the other in which to seat the class to listen to the broadcasts and write criticisms at the conclusion of each speech. Even though the talks do not actually go on the air, this experience is practical.

If broadcasting studios are not available, the school auditorium or other suitable rooms and loud-speaker systems may be used. If the microphone is set up behind a curtain or off-stage, the class being seated in the auditorium or an adjoining room, excellent results may be obtained.

Explanation of Radio Speaking

Radio speech may be dramatization, debate, discussion, or any of the many different types of speech presented over the radio or on television. The present assignment is concerned with the radio speech. Its chief characteristics are its strict adherence to rigid time limits, and language suitable to an audience of average people. Generally radio speeches are read, thus enabling the speaker to meet these requisites of time and diction.

The requirements of radio speaking are a pleasing voice, proper speech construction, good English, correct pronunciation, clear enunciation, and cooperation among all concerned in the broadcast.

Willingness to rehearse and promptness at the studio are of major importance. The person who is tardy or who arrives only five minutes before time to go on the air has no business near a radio station.

Suggested Topics for Radio Speaking

1. Agriculture.
2. Foreign problems.
3. Educational problems.
4. Safety.
5. National parks.
6. Business opportunities.
7. Baseball leagues.
8. Low-income workers.
9. Aeronautics and the future.
10. Neurotics.
11. Recreation problems.
12. Art.
13. The armed forces.
14. Service organizations.
15. Health problems.
16. Automobiles.
17. Public utilities.
18. Leisure time.
19. Science.
20. Speaker's choice.

How to Choose a Topic for a Radio Speech

Follow all the principles for selecting any subject, but keep in mind that a radio audience is the most diverse and varied in the world. Hence, unless you deliberately intend your speech for a limited group, select a topic that can be presented to cross sections of listeners. All the topics suggested above are very general; they should be restricted to some single phase that interests you and can be developed interestingly.

How to Prepare a Radio Speech

All the principles governing preparation of the type of speech you intend to present apply here. Decide what kind of speech you will present, and in preparing it give special attention to details and correctness. No excuses can be made for errors when you have a written copy in front of you. The speech should be typed double-spaced for easy reading.

The language in a radio speech should be simple, understandable, and conversational in style. Use words that are clear, vivid, and descriptive so that you can build word pictures in the minds of your listeners. Your sentences should be short, not over fifteen or twenty words each at the most. Avoid trite and overworked words and phrases. Generally speaking, strive for language that in effect makes the listener feel that you are having a lively and interesting conversation with him.

Submit the final draft of your speech to your instructor for approval. After the preparation is completed, numerous rehearsals will be required before you are ready to step before the microphone. If possible, practice with a microphone while a friend listens critically and offers suggestions for improvement. The use of a recording machine for practice is helpful. If desirable, after several rehearsals you may write time signals in the margin of your paper to tell you where you should be at the end of two, three, four minutes, etc. These may be checked with the studio clock while you are presenting your speech.

How to Present a Radio Speech

Ordinarily, radio speeches are presented with the thought that the people who are listening will be scattered far and wide throughout the nation, possibly the world. They may be congregated in groups of two, three, or four, or there may be only one person in a home listening to a speech. Your presentation should be so tempered that it meets the situation of every listener. Ask yourself how you would speak if you were to come before these small groups in person.

Remember that only your voice will be heard. This means that there must be enough animation, clarity, force, and emphasis to give interest. On television, of course, you are in full view for all to see and hear. This calls attention to posture, gestures, bodily action, and appearance.

In giving your speech, let each sheet of manuscript drop from your hand to the floor as you finish reading it. Avoid rustling your paper in any way. Do not cough, sneeze, clear your throat, or shout into the mike. Keep a uniform distance from the mike all the time you are speaking. This prevents fading or sudden increases in volume. If you feel like gesturing, go ahead. It will give life to your speech. Just be sure to talk into the microphone all the time, with or without gestures. If you stand about ten inches from it, you will be close enough, provided the mechanism is sensitive. The best plan is to rehearse with a live microphone and thus be fully prepared.

BIBLIOGRAPHY

Baird, *Discuss.*, chap. 18.
Borchers & Wise, chap. 18.
Brigance, *Speech Comm.*, chap. 9.
Brigance, *Speech Comp.*, pp. 294-299.
Buehler, part 2, chap. 7.
Butler, chap. 10.
Carlile, complete book.
Crocker, *Bus. & Prof. Speech*, chap. 29.

Crocker, *Pub. Spkg.*, pp. 367-379.
Dolman, chap. 19.
Gilman, Aly, & Reid, chap. 21.
Glasgow, chap. 8.
Hibbitt, chap. 22.
Monroe, *Prin. & Types*, chap. 26.
Monroe, *Prin.*, chap. 8.
Powers, *Fund.*, chap. 26.

PROJECT 37

THE PANEL DISCUSSION

There is no better method of resolving the world's problems than by "talking them over." The panel discussion, when operating successfully, utilizes this method. It is democracy at work. Every citizen and certainly every student should have the experience of deliberately sitting down in the company of other persons to find the answers to problems of mutual concern.

Explanation of the Panel Discussion

A panel discussion occurs when a group of persons sit down together to try to solve a problem by pooling their knowledge and thus arriving at decisions satisfactory to the majority. If they reach these decisions, their purpose is fulfilled. This requires that the members of the panel have *open minds and a willingness and desire to hear other viewpoints, opinions, and evidence.* Thus by gathering all possible information (facts) and by pooling it, the group can examine a problem bit by bit, point by point, and arrive at a logical solution. No one should consent to be on a panel while harboring preconceived ideas, prejudices, and opinions which he is unwilling to change in the light of evidence he does not have. Open-mindedness is the most valuable asset a panel speaker or anyone else can possess. This does not mean that he is vacillating but rather that he easily and gladly changes his mind when confronted by information which perhaps he did not know was in existence.

Panels vary greatly in number of members; however, if there are too many, progress tends to be slow and laborious. It is, therefore, advisable to limit membership to a maximum of five or six persons besides the chairman.

Occasions for a panel discussion are as numerous as the problems that face any group of people. Every club, every society or organization, has recourse to the panel as a method of problem solving. Naturally, if an organization has a large membership, its problems will be submitted to committees which will in turn attack them by the discussion method, that is to say, the panel. It is not necessary to have an audience for every panel discussion. Today the radio often features the panel as a public service. However, certain radio programs dominated by sarcasm, acrimony, and quibbling do not represent true discussion, because they lack the quality of open-mindedness and a sincere desire to solve a problem.

Suggested Problems for Panel Discussion

(Note that the topics are phrased in the form of questions, since questions imply that their answers are to be found in the form of solutions.)

1. What is the most desirable minimum age for military training?
2. How may more people be encouraged to take V.D. tests?
3. How may government efficiency be improved?
4. How may crime be controlled?
5. How may political bosses be controlled?
6. How may more educational facilities be offered to low-income students?
7. What should be done to assist Indians now on reservations?
8. What should be done to improve college curriculums?
9. What should be done about cheating in college?
10. What should be the policy relative to paying athletes or granting them special privileges?
11. How should labor unions be improved?
12. How should sororities and fraternities be improved?
13. What should be done to improve the attendance at college functions?
14. What should students do in regard to race discrimination?
15. Should courses in marriage be required in college?
16. Should teachers join teachers' unions affiliated with national organizations?
17. Should all physically able male college students be required to enter the R.O.T.C.?
18. What should be done to improve freshman orientation week?

19. Should the government assist young married couples with subsidies when children are born?
20. Panel's choice.

How to Choose a Problem for Panel Discussion

If the problem is not assigned, the panel should meet under the leadership of the chairman and consider various problems, selection of a discussion topic being made by majority vote. The selection should be based on interest to the members and the availability of material for research and study. If the discussion is to be conducted before a group, audience interests should be considered. In any case the group should select a question they are capable of discussing adequately. In other words, technical problems should be avoided. If the general problem selected is too broad for adequate treatment in the allotted time, narrow it suitably.

How to Prepare for a Panel Discussion

Participants should give careful thought to the purpose of a panel discussion—*solving a problem*. They should prepare their material with this purpose uppermost. Their attitude should be that of a farmer who sees a strange plant growing in his field. What should he do about it? Is it harmful? Is it valuable? Should he dig it out by the roots or cut it off? Who can tell him what kind of plant it is? In other words, the student should not jump at conclusions immediately on selecting a problem, but find out all he can about the question under discussion and then make up his mind regarding what opinions he will hold and what he should do about them.

Let us assume that the problem has been selected and the panel members are ready to begin searching for possible solutions. The problem selected is: What should be done to decrease the number of divorces? Here are steps the participants may take in arriving at possible answers.
1. Study the effects of divorce, both good and bad. Ask your teacher and the librarian to help you locate sources of information.
2. Find out what caused these good and bad effects.
3. What requirements should solutions to the problem meet? For example,
    A. Any solution must be fair to both the man and the woman, and to the children, if any.
    B. Any solution must be legal and constitutional.
    C. Any solution must be acceptable to the church, the community, etc.
4. State several tentative solutions to the problem, and list their advantages and disadvantages. (Remember that you must not be prejudiced in your solutions. You will soon say to the other members, "Here are my ideas, and their good and bad points. This is what I believe on the basis of the information I could find. However, I'm willing to change my views if your information indicates I should.")
5. Now select the solution you think best.
6. Suggest ways and means of putting it into action.

Now you are ready to meet with the other members of the panel to see what they have discovered. Obviously you will not all have the same information, because you did not all read the same sources and talk to the same people. Your possible solutions will be different too. Nevertheless, you pool your knowledge; and after thoroughly talking it over and examining all the data carefully, you decide on possible solutions that a majority of the panel agree on. These solutions represent cooperative effort.

How to Present a Panel Discussion

In presenting a panel you meet as a group and discuss the information and ideas of each member. To do this effectively each one must desire to find mutual answers, not to propound and seek adoption of his personal ideas and solutions. This open-mindedness is the most important aspect of the discussion.

The members of the panel should sit in a semicircle or around a large table, so that each person can easily see everyone else during the discussion. The chairman sits near the middle of the group. If there is an audience, the panel members must be seated so that they are visible to the listeners. The speakers must be sure that their remarks can be heard easily by everyone present, and they should direct their voices toward the audience as well as toward the panel.

Each panel member must remember that he is neither to dominate the occasion nor to withdraw and say little or nothing, and further that he is not to become angry, impolite, sarcastic, or acrimonious. He will, however, be earnest and sincere, even persistent if necessary. The chairman, in turn, should insist on a policy of fairness. He must encourage the more timid to speak their minds, and promote harmony and good will among the group. He may permit some digression from the main question, but he will direct the discussion in such a way that the main problem is explored. He notes the passing of time and makes certain that the discussion progresses rapidly enough to be completed within the allotted time.

To begin the discussion the chairman makes brief introductory remarks in which he mentions the reasons for discussing the topic. He introduces members of the panel (if there is an audience) and tells where each comes from, his occupation, and anything else appropriate. The discussion should be entirely informal throughout—a spontaneous give-and-take with free and easy questions, answers, and contributions from everyone without any prompting from the chairman. However, he may call on a member if he thinks it necessary to do so.

The points to discuss should be developed in the following order in informal talk:

1. Define the terms. Be sure you all agree on what you are talking about.
2. Talk about what the problem is.
3. Discuss its causes.
4. Set up standards which any solutions should meet.
5. Advance tentative solutions or conclusions, and state advantages and disadvantages of each one.
6. Select one tentative solution as best.
7. Decide how it can be put into action.
8. The chairman should then summarize briefly what the panel has accomplished.
9. The chairman may permit the audience (if there is one) to ask the panel members questions; he should rule out those that obviously have no bearing on the discussion or are out of order.
10. The chairman concludes the meeting with a brief summary.

BIBLIOGRAPHY

Baird, *Discuss.*, pp. 197-208.

Borchers & Wise, chap. 14.

Brigance, *Speech Comm.*, chap. 8.

Butler, chap. 12.

Ewbank & Auer, part 4.

Glasgow, pp. 211-221, 224, 225.

Hibbitt, chap. 11.

McBurney & Hance, pp. 287-297.

Monroe, *Prin. & Types*, chaps. 27-29.

Monroe, *Prin.*, chap. 6.

Murray, pp. 59-61.

O'Neill, chap. 13.

Runion, chap. 6.

Thonssen & Gilkinson, chap. 24.

Name . . . . Date . . . . Type of speech . . . .

Specific purpose of this speech . . . .

. . . . No. of sources required . . . . . .

Sentence outline: 125-200 words.   Time limit: 30 minutes if time is available.

Speaking notes: Have figures, facts, sources, etc., available.

TITLE

INTRODUCTION

BODY

CONCLUSION

INSTRUCTOR'S COMMENTS

  Clarity of purpose . . . .

  Gesture-action-eye contact . . . .

  Language . . . .

  Voice . . . .

  Enthusiasm and vigor . . . .

  Self-confidence . . . .

  Organization . . . .

  Introduction and conclusion . . . .

  Grade . . . .
                        (List sources on back of page as indicated)

PRINTED SOURCES OF INFORMATION

Give complete information for each source.

1. Author's name . . . .

    Title of article . . . .

    Book or magazine containing article . . . .

    . . . . Date of publication . . . .

    Chapters and/or pages containing material . . . .

2. Author's name . . . .

    Title of article . . . .

    Book or magazine containing article . . . .

    . . . . Date of publication . . . .

    Chapters and/or pages containing material . . . .

3. Author's name . . . .

    Title of article . . . .

    Book or magazine containing article . . . .

    . . . . Date of publication . . . .

    Chapters and/or pages containing material . . . .

INTERVIEW SOURCES OF INFORMATION

1. Name of person interviewed. . . . . Date of interview . . . .

    His title, position, and occupation . . . .

    . . . .

    Why is he an authority on the subject? Be specific. . . . .

    . . . .

2. Name of person interviewed. . . . . Date of interview . . . .

    His title, position, and occupation . . . .

    . . . .

    Why is he an authority on the subject? Be specific. . . . .

    . . . .

3. Name of person interviewed. . . . . Date of interview . . . .

    His title, position, and occupation . . . .

    . . . .

    Why is he an authority on the subject? Be specific. . . . .

    . . . .

THE SYMPOSIUM

Explanation of the Symposium

The symposium is a type of discussion that is being used more and more as a means of informing and enlightening the public. It is a method of presenting representative aspects of a problem. Usually three or four speakers talk about one general question, each speaker presenting his views on a particular aspect. A chairman acts as moderator and leader. He synchronizes the different speeches to produce unification of ideas rather than a series of unrelated lectures. Each speaker has the responsibility of fitting his remarks to the main question. The time allotted each speaker is the same, but it may vary from a few minutes to fifteen or twenty each if time permits. Following the speeches the participants may hold a panel discussion, after which the audience may be invited to ask questions of the speakers. The complete program may last as much as an hour and a half or more if the audience is active and the speakers capable, and if there is time.

Occasions for a symposium may be the meeting of a club, a society, a religious, fraternal, or business organization, an educational group, or any civic gathering or other assemblage. Today radio utilizes the symposium frequently on certain types of programs.

Suggested Topics for a Symposium

1. How may the U.N. be improved?
2. What should be done to insure permanent peace in the Orient?
3. What should be done to promote progress in Mexico?
4. What should be done with atomic power?
5. Should a national lottery be established?
6. What should be done to improve American-Russian relations?
7. What are the aspects of a federal world government?
8. Should the United States have compulsory military training?
9. Should we have federal aid for education?
10. Should colleges require their faculties to sign noncommunist pledges?
11. What should be done to improve our judicial system?
12. Should the closed shop be prohibited by law?
13. Should college scholarships in the form of federal assistance be given to all high-school graduates with outstanding records?
14. Should teachers be required to have college degrees?
15. What should be done to improve city government?
16. What should be done to decrease automobile accidents?
17. Should moving pictures have to pass national boards of censorship?
18. Should federal laws be enacted to control rain-makers?
19. Should comic books be controlled by national censorship boards?
20. Symposium's choice.

How to Choose a Topic

Members of a symposium should meet with their chairman and by general agreement decide on a proposition, preferably one that is interesting to everyone. Be sure that your selection is one about which you can secure information by interviews and reading. The topic to be discussed should then be divided by mutual agreement among three or more speakers so that each one presents a different aspect of it.

How to Prepare a Symposium

The individual speakers should prepare their speeches in accordance with the principles governing the type of speech they plan to present. All the steps of preparation should be included, from audience analysis to rehearsal, and the time limit observed closely.

The chairman should be well prepared on the entire subject because he will direct discussion on it. He determines the order of speakers and makes brief introductory remarks which include these facts: (1) a short history and statement of the proposition, (2) reasons for its discussion, (3) relationship and importance of the topic to the audience, (4) definition of terms of the proposition, (5) names, subjects, and order of the speakers, and (6) the manner in which the symposium will be conducted. The chairman should familiarize himself generally with the point of view each speaker will take, and make a brief summary both at the conclusion of the speeches and after the questions from the audience.

How to Present a Symposium

Throughout the entire symposium good speech practices should of course be followed. The members of the symposium are seated side by side with the chairman at one end or in the middle. The chairman makes his introductory remarks, introduces members of the symposium, and presents the speakers and their topics in order. At the conclusion of the speeches he briefly summarizes the ideas which have been presented, after which the symposium may be continued according to one of the following alternatives:

1. The speakers form a panel for a limited time and discuss the ideas presented. The chairman then summarizes briefly and adjourns the meeting.
2. The speakers form a panel as above, after which the audience is permitted to question them for a limited or unlimited time by directing questions through the chairman. The chairman concludes as before.
3. The panel may be omitted and the audience permitted to question the speakers immediately, after which the chairman briefly summarizes the forum and adjourns the meeting.

BIBLIOGRAPHY

Baird, *Discuss.*, pp. 208-213.
Borchers & Wise, chap. 14.
Brigance, *Speech Comm.*, chap. 8.
Butler, chap. 12.
Ewbank & Auer, part 4.
Glasglow, pp. 222-224.

Hibbitt, chap. 11.
McBurney & Hance, pp. 299-302.
Monroe, *Prin. & Types*, chaps. 27-29.
Monroe, *Prin.* chap. 6.
O'Neill, chap. 13.
Thonssen & Gilkinson, chap. 24.

SPEECH OUTLINE, PROJECT 38

Name . . . . Date . . . . .Type of speech . . . .

Specific purpose of this speech . . . .

. . . . .No. of sources required . . . . . .

Outline: Prepare one to insure proper organization; not to be handed in.

Time limit: 5-6 minutes.   Speaking notes: None for speaker;   whatever necessary for chairman.

TITLE

INTRODUCTION

BODY

CONCLUSION

INSTRUCTOR'S COMMENTS

Clarity of purpose. . . . .

Gesture-action-eye contact . . . .

Language . . . .

Voice. . . . .

Enthusiasm and vigor . . . .

Self-confidence. . . . .

Organization . . . .

Introduction and conclusion . . . .

Grade . . . .

(List sources on back of page as indicated)

(153)

PRINTED SOURCES OF INFORMATION

Give complete information for each source.

1. Author's name . . . .

   Title of article . . . .

   Book or magazine containing article . . . .

   . . . . Date of publication . . . .

   Chapters and/or pages containing material . . . .

2. Author's name . . . .

   Title of article . . . .

   Book or magazine containing article . . . .

   . . . . Date of publication . . . .

   Chapters and/or pages containing material . . . .

3. Author's name . . . .

   Title of article . . . .

   Book or magazine containing article . . . .

   . . . . Date of publication . . . .

   Chapters and/or pages containing material . . . .

INTERVIEW SOURCES OF INFORMATION

1. Name of person interviewed . . . . Date of interview . . . .

   His title, position, and occupation . . . .

   . . . .

   Why is he an authority on the subject? Be specific. . . . .

   . . . .

2. Name of person interviewed . . . . Date of interview . . . .

   His title, position, and occupation . . . .

   . . . .

   Why is he an authority on the subject? Be specific. . . . .

   . . . .

3. Name of person interviewed . . . . Date of interview . . . .

   His title, position, and occupation . . . .

   . . . .

   Why is he an authority on the subject? Be specific. . . . .

   . . . .

PROJECT 39

THE LECTURE FORUM

Speakers seldom know how many unanswered questions they leave in the minds of their listeners, because the hearers have no chance to voice their questions. Speakers can be more helpful to their listeners if they remain on stage following their lecture to answer questions from the audience.

Most students do not receive training in answering questions about the material they present in speeches; hence, when they are confronted with a question period after a speech they are in danger of handling themselves and their audience awkwardly. This lecture-forum type of speech, designed to provide experience in speaking as well as in answering questions, should be both enlightening and challenging to student speakers.

Explanation of the Lecture Forum

The purpose of the lecturer who is to have a forum follow his speech generally is to inform his hearers on a worth-while subject, or to convince. For a lecture forum the speaker should discuss an informative subject.

The lecture forum demands that the speaker be better informed than any member of his audience, and further that he be capable of handling questions from an audience.

Occasions for the lecture forum occur whenever speeches are given before committees, business groups, church organizations, civic audiences, educational meetings, fraternal orders, and the like. There is almost no limit to occasions for a forum.

Suggested Topics for a Lecture Forum
1. How may our foreign relations be improved?
2. The problem of juvenile gangs.
3. The influence of motion pictures on morals.
4. The book market.
5. Making medicine safe.
6. Telecasting sports events.
7. Pure-food laws.
8. Owning a home versus renting.
9. The problem of the feeble-minded.
10. The future of atomic-driven machines.
11. Beneath the ocean.
12. The possibility of landing on the moon.
13. Infantile paralysis.
14. New methods in selling.
15. Alcoholics Anonymous.
16. Speech correction clinics in colleges.
17. The problem of suicides.
18. The best vacation spots in the United States.
19. Industrial schools.
20. Speaker's choice.

How to Choose a Topic for a Lecture Forum

You will be expected to know your subject unusually well, because you will open the meeting to questions after you have spoken. Choose a topic of interest to you and your listeners, one about which you can secure plenty of information.

How to Prepare for a Lecture Forum

Since this is an informative speech, reread Project 12, "The Speech to Inform—Any Subject." Follow it closely.

How to Present a Lecture Forum

Project 12 tells you how to present your speech, but not how to conduct the period of questioning from your audience.

Immediately after the conclusion of your lecture the audience is told by the chairman or yourself that they may question you. In making this announcement several points should be explained politely but thoroughly, such as:

1. Questions should be confined to the material presented in the lecture.
2. Only questions are in order, unless you wish to permit short speeches on the subject. In that case, announce a definite time limit for the speeches. For the classroom one minute is enough; for large public gatherings two minutes is adequate.
3. If the audience is small and informal, do not request that they stand while asking their questions. If it is large, they should stand. This applies to you, too.
4. Announce the time allowed for questioning; don't make it too long. You can always extend it if questions are coming briskly when the time is up. On the other hand, do not hold the audience for the complete time if it is obvious that they have no more questions.
5. Answer the questions in the order in which they are asked. If two persons speak at once, indicate which one is to speak first. In a small informal group the audience should be urged to speak out rather than to raise their hands and wait to be called on.

If a question is asked that you do not feel qualified to answer, tell your interrogator that you do not have the information necessary to give him a reliable answer. But if you do not know the answer because you are poorly prepared you will quickly lose the confidence and respect of your audience — and you should.

If a question is asked which does not pertain to the subject, say politely that it is beyond the scope of your talk. Should you by chance have information which enables you to answer it, state briefly that the question is somewhat far afield but you can answer it, and then make a very brief reply. Do not let this take you off your subject for more than a moment.

If a heckler troubles you, handle him courteously but firmly. Read the project dealing with heckling speeches.

If questions are obscure and long drawn-out, rephrase them, but ask the questioner whether your rewording expresses what he wants to know. At other times it may be necessary to ask for a restatement of an inquiry. Always do this when you do not hear or understand the question clearly.

Observe acceptable speaking practices throughout your speech and the period following. Maintain an alert and friendly attitude. Do not become ruffled when you meet obvious disagreement or criticism. Simply explain your position firmly but courteously. Do not engage in a debate or an exchange of unfriendly remarks and accusations. Dismiss the matter and go on to the next question. If some of the questions are "hot"—and they will be—keep your head, add a touch of humor to cool them off if it seems advisable, then reply as capably as you can.

When you are ready to turn the meeting back to the chairman, conclude with appropriate remarks in which you sincerely express your pleasure in having addressed the audience. Also compliment them for their interest in the subject.

BIBLIOGRAPHY

Baird, *Discuss.*, chap. 16.
Borchers & Wise, chap. 14.
Butler, chap. 12.
Ewbank & Auer, part 4.
Glasgow, p. 226.

Hibbitt, chap. 11.
McBurney & Hance, pp. 302-305.
Monroe, *Prin. & Types*, chaps. 27-29.
Monroe, *Prin.*, chap. 6.
Thonssen & Gilkinson, chap. 24.

SPEECH OUTLINE, PROJECT 39

Name . . . . Date . . . . Type of speech . . . .

Specific purpose of this speech . . . .

. . . . No. of sources required . . . . . .

Sentence outline: 75-150 words.   Speaking notes: 15-word limit.

Time limit: 7-8 minutes for the speech, followed by 5-minute question period.

TITLE

INTRODUCTION

BODY

CONCLUSION

INSTRUCTOR'S COMMENTS

Clarity of purpose . . . .

Gesture-action-eye contact . . . .

Language . . . .

Voice . . . .

Enthusiasm and vigor . . . .

Self-confidence . . . .

Organization . . . .

Introduction and conclusion . . . .

Grade . . . .
                    (List sources on back of page as indicated)

PRINTED SOURCES OF INFORMATION

Give complete information for each source.

1. Author's name . . . .
   Title of article . . . .
   Book or magazine containing article . . . .
   . . . . Date of publication . . . .
   Chapters and/or pages containing material . . . .
2. Author's name . . . .
   Title of article . . . .
   Book or magazine containing article . . . .
   . . . . Date of publication . . . .
   Chapters and/or pages containing material . . . .
3. Author's name . . . .
   Title of article . . . .
   Book or magazine containing article . . . .
   . . . . Date of publication . . . .
   Chapters and/or pages containing material . . . .

INTERVIEW SOURCES OF INFORMATION

1. Name of person interviewed. . . . . Date of interview . . . .
   His title, position, and occupation . . . .
   . . . .
   Why is he an authority on the subject? Be specific . . . .
   . . . .
2. Name of person interviewed . . . . Date of interview . . . .
   His title, position, and occupation . . . .
   . . . .
   Why is he an authority on the subject? Be specific . . . .
   . . . .
3. Name of person interviewed . . . . Date of interview . . . .
   His title, position, and occupation . . . .
   . . . .
   Why is he an authority on the subject? Be specific . . . .
   . . . .

BIBLIOGRAPHY

Baird, A. Craig, *Discussion: Principles and Types*, McGraw-Hill, 1943.

Baird, A. Craig (ed.), *Representative American Speeches*, Wilson, 1949-1950, 1950-1951.

Baird, A. Craig, and Knower, F.H., *General Speech*, McGraw-Hill, 1949.

Baker, James Thompson, *The Short Speech*, Prentice-Hall, 1928.

Book Review Digest, H. W. Wilson.

Borchers, Gladys L., and Wise, C.M., *Modern Speech*, Harcourt, Brace, 1947.

Borden, Richard C., *Public Speaking as Listeners Like It*, Harper, 1935.

Brigance, William Norwood, *Speech Communication*, Appleton-Century-Crofts, 1947.

Brigance, William Norwood, *Speech Composition*, Appleton-Century-Crofts, 1947.

Brigance, William Norwood, *The Spoken Word*, Crofts, 1929.

Brigance, William Norwood, and Immel, R.K., *Speechmaking Principles and Practice*, Appleton-Century-Crofts, 1938.

Bryant, Donald C., and Wallace, K.R., *Fundamentals of Public Speaking*, Appleton-Century-Crofts, 1947.

Bryant, Donald C., and Wallace, K.R., *Oral Communication*, Appleton-Century-Crofts, 1948.

Buehler, E. C., *You and Your Speeches*, Allen Press, 1947.

Butler, Jessie Haver, *Time to Speak Up*, Harper, 1946.

Carlile, John S., *Production and Direction of Radio Programs*, Prentice-Hall, 1939.

Carnegie, Dale, *Public Speaking and Influencing Men in Business*, Association Press, 1937.

Crocker, Lionel, *Business and Professional Speech*, Ronald, 1951.

Crocker, Lionel, *Public Speaking for College Students*, American Book, 1941; 2nd ed., 1950.

Dolman, John, Jr., *A Handbook of Public Speaking*, Harcourt, Brace, 1944.

Eisenson, Jon, *Psychology of Speech*, Appleton-Century-Crofts, 1938.

Ewbank, Henry Lee, and Auer, J.J., *Discussion and Debate*, Appleton-Century-Crofts, rev. ed., 1941.

Fessenden, Seth A., and Thompson, W.N., *Basic Experiences in Speech*, Prentice-Hall, 1951.

Gilman, Wilbur E., Aly, Bower, and Reid, L.D., *The Fundamentals of Speaking*, Macmillan, 1951.

Glasgow, George M., *Dynamic Public Speaking*, Harper, 1950.

Goode, Kenneth M., *How to Turn People into Gold*, Harper, 1929.

Gray, Giles W., and Braden, W.W., *Public Speaking Principles and Practice*, Harper, 1951.

Hibbitt, George W., *How to Speak Effectively on All Occasions*, Garden City, 1947.

Hickerson, J.M. (ed.), *How I Made the Sale That Did the Most for Me*, Prentice-Hall, 1951.

Hollingworth, H.L., *Psychology of the Audience*, American Book, 1935.

Huston, Alfred D., and Sandberg, R.A., *Everyday Business Speech*, Prentice-Hall, 1943.

Ivey, Paul W., *Successful Salesmanship*, Prentice-Hall, 1947.

Lowery, Sara, and Johnson, G. E., *Interpretive Reading Techniques and Selections*, Appleton-Century-Crofts, 1942.

McBurney, James H., and Hance, K. G., *Principles and Methods of Discussion*, Harper, 1939.

Meiers, Mildred, and Knapp, Jack, *Thesaurus of Humor*, Crown, 1940.

Miller, Clyde R., *Process of Persuasion*, Crown, 1946.

Monroe, Alan H., *Principles and Types of Speech*, Scott, Foresman, 1939; 3rd ed., 1949.

Monroe, Alan H., *Principles of Speech*, Brief Edition, Scott, Foresman, 1945.

Muller, Helen M., *Still More Jokes*, Wilson, 1935.

Murray, Elwood, *The Speech Personality*, Lippincott, 1944.

Norvelle, Lee, and Smith, R. G., *Speaking Effectively*, Longmans, Green, 1948.

Oliver, Robert T., and Cortright, R. L., *New Training for Effective Speech*, Dryden, rev. ed., 1950.

Oliver, Robert T., and others, *New Training for Effective Speech*, Dryden, 1946.

Oliver, Robert T., Dickey, D. C., and Zelko, H.P., *Essentials of Communicative Speech*, Dryden, 1949.

O'Neill, James M., *Extemporaneous Speaking*, Harper, 1946.

O'Neill, James M., and Weaver, A.T., *The Elements of Speech*, Longmans, Green, 1936.

Parrish, Wayland Maxfield, *Reading Aloud*, Nelson, 1932.

Parrish, Wayland Maxfield, *Speaking in Public*, Scribner, 1947.

Powers, David Guy, *Fundamentals of Speech*, McGraw-Hill, 1951.

Printers Ink Editors and Contributors, *Sales Idea Book*, Funk & Wagnalls, 1949.

Quarterly Journal of Speech, Speech Association of America.

Rango, Robert (ed.), *The Good Humor Book*, Harvest House, 1944.

Rogers, Lawrence W., *How to Talk Effectively*, Joseph F. Wagoner, 1947.

Roth, Charles B., *Secrets of Closing Sales*, Prentice-Hall, 2nd ed., 1947.

Runion, Howard L., *Essentials of Effective Public Speaking*, Longmans, Green, 1948.

Russell, Frederic A., and Beach, F.H., *Textbook of Salesmanship*, McGraw-Hill, 1949.

Sandford, William Phillips, and Yeager, W.H., *Practical Business Speaking*, McGraw-Hill, 1937.

Sandford, William Phillips, and Yeager, W.H., *Principles of Effective Speaking*, 3rd ed., Nelson, 1934; 4th ed., Ronald, 1942.

Sarett, Lew, and Foster, W. T., *Basic Principles of Speech*, Houghton Mifflin, rev. ed., 1946.

Schubert, Leland, *A Guide for Oral Communication*, Prentice-Hall, 1948.

Soper, Paul L., *Basic Public Speaking*, Oxford, 1949.

Sutton, Kelso, *The Technique of Selling*, Gregg, 1949.

Thompson, A.R., *Handbook of Public Speaking*, Harper, rev. ed., 1949.

Thonssen, Lester, and Gilkinson, Howard, *Basic Training in Speech*, Heath, 1947.

Thonssen, Lester, and Scanlan, Ross, *Speech Preparation and Delivery*, Lippincott, 1942.

Tresidder, Argus, *Reading to Others*, Scott, Foresman, 1940.

Weaver, Andrew Thomas, *Speech, Forms and Principles*, Longmans, Green, 1942.

Whiting, Percy H., *The Five Great Rules of Selling*, McGraw-Hill, 1947.

Williamson, Arleigh B., *Speaking in Public*, Prentice-Hall, 1929.

Williamson, Arleigh B., and others, *Speaking in Public*, Prentice-Hall, 2nd ed., 1948.

Winans, James A., *Speech Making*, Appleton-Century-Crofts, 1938.

Wise, Claude Merton, and others, *Foundations of Speech*, Prentice-Hall, 1941.

Woolbert, Charles H., and Weaver, A.T., *Better Speech*, Harcourt, Brace, 1929.

Yeager, Willard Hayes, *Effective Speaking for Every Occasion*, Prentice-Hall, 1940.

REPORT ON A SPEECH HEARD IN PUBLIC

Student's Name . . . . Class and Section . . . .

1. Name, title, and position of speaker: . . . .

. . . .

2. Subject: . . . .

3. Occasion: . . . .

4. Place: . . . . Time:. . . . . . Date: . . . .

5. Purpose of speech: to inform ☐ ;   to stimulate and arouse ☐ ;   to convince ☐ ; to get action ☐ ;   to entertain ☐ .

6. Explain the introduction and conclusion as to the type used. . . . .

. . . .

. . . .

7. What basic appeals did the speaker use? . . . .

. . . .

. . . .

8. Was the proof logical? emotional? personal? Explain. . . . .

. . . .

. . . .

9. Were sources of evidence stated accurately? Explain. . . . .

. . . .

. . . .

10. Describe the speaker's platform behavior. . . . .

. . . .

. . . .

11. Describe the speaker's use of language. . . . .

. . . .

. . . .

12. What was your reaction to the speech? Be specific. . . . .

. . . .

. . . .

(Use form on back for reporting another speech)

REPORT ON A SPEECH HEARD IN PUBLIC

Student's Name .... Class and Section ....

1. Name, title and position of speaker: ....

   ....

2. Subject: ....

3. Occasion: ....

4. Place: .... Time: ...... Date: ....

5. Purpose of speech: to inform ☐ ;   to stimulate and arouse ☐ ;   to convince ☐ ;
   to get action ☐ ;   to entertain ☐ .

6. Explain the introduction and conclusion as to types used. ....

   ....

   ....

7. What basic appeals did the speaker use? ....

   ....

   ....

8. Was the proof logical? emotional? personal? Explain. ....

   ....

   ....

9. Were sources of evidence stated accurately? Explain. ....

   ....

   ....

10. Describe the speaker's platform behavior. ....

    ....

    ....

11. Describe the speaker's use of language. ....

    ....

    ....

12. What was your reaction to the speech? Be specific. ....

    ....

    ....

REPORT ON A SPEECH HEARD IN PUBLIC

Student's Name . . . . Class and Section . . . .

1. Name, title, and position of speaker: . . . .

. . . .

2. Subject: . . . .

3. Occasion: . . . .

4. Place: . . . . Time:. . . . . . Date: . . . .

5. Purpose of speech: to inform ☐ ;   to stimulate and arouse ☐ ;   to convince ☐ ;
   to get action ☐ ;   to entertain ☐ .

6. Explain the introduction and conclusion as to the type used. . . . .

. . . .

. . . .

7. What basic appeals did the speaker use? . . . .

. . . .

. . . .

8. Was the proof logical? emotional? personal? Explain. . . . .

. . . .

. . . .

9. Were sources of evidence stated accurately? Explain. . . . .

. . . .

. . . .

10. Describe the speaker's platform behavior. . . . .

. . . .

. . . .

11. Describe the speaker's use of language. . . . .

. . . .

. . . .

12. What was your reaction to the speech? Be specific. . . . .

. . . .

. . . .

(Use form on back for reporting another speech)

REPORT ON A SPEECH HEARD IN PUBLIC

Student's Name ....Class and Section ....

1. Name, title and position of speaker: ....

    ....

2. Subject: ....

3. Occasion: ....

4. Place: .... Time: ...... Date: ....

5. Purpose of speech: to inform ☐ ;   to stimulate and arouse ☐ ;   to convince ☐ ;
    to get action ☐ ;   to entertain ☐ .

6. Explain the introduction and conclusion as to types used. ....

    ....

    ....

7. What basic appeals did the speaker use? ....

    ....

    ....

8. Was the proof logical? emotional? personal? Explain. ....

    ....

    ....

9. Were sources of evidence stated accurately? Explain. ....

    ....

    ....

10. Describe the speaker's platform behavior. ....

    ....

    ....

11. Describe the speaker's use of language. ....

    ....

    ....

12. What was your reaction to the speech? Be specific. ....

    ....

    ....

REPORT ON A SPEECH HEARD IN PUBLIC

Student's Name . . . . Class and Section . . . .

1. Name, title, and position of speaker: . . . .

. . . .

2. Subject: . . . .

3. Occasion: . . . .

4. Place: . . . . Time: . . . . . . Date: . . . .

5. Purpose of speech: to inform ☐ ;   to stimulate and arouse ☐ ;   to convince ☐ ;
to get action ☐ ;   to entertain ☐ .

6. Explain the introduction and conclusion as to the type used. . . . .

. . . .

. . . .

7. What basic appeals did the speaker use? . . . .

. . . .

. . . .

8. Was the proof logical? emotional? personal? Explain. . . . .

. . . .

. . . .

9. Were sources of evidence stated accurately? Explain. . . . .

. . . .

. . . .

10. Describe the speaker's platform behavior. . . . .

. . . .

. . . .

11. Describe the speaker's use of language. . . . .

. . . .

. . . .

12. What was your reaction to the speech? Be specific. . . . .

. . . .

. . . .

(Use form on back for reporting another speech)

REPORT ON A SPEECH HEARD IN PUBLIC

Student's Name . . . . Class and Section . . . .

1. Name, title and position of speaker: . . . .

. . . .

2. Subject: . . . .

3. Occasion: . . . .

4. Place: . . . . Time: . . . . . . Date: . . . .

5. Purpose of speech: to inform ☐ ;   to stimulate and arouse ☐ ;   to convince ☐ ;
to get action ☐ ;   to entertain ☐ .

6. Explain the introduction and conclusion as to types used. . . . .

. . . .

. . . .

7. What basic appeals did the speaker use? . . . .

. . . .

. . . .

8. Was the proof logical? emotional? personal? Explain. . . . .

. . . .

. . . .

9. Were sources of evidence stated accurately? Explain. . . . .

. . . .

. . . .

10. Describe the speaker's platform behavior. . . . .

. . . .

. . . .

11. Describe the speaker's use of language. . . . .

. . . .

. . . .

12. What was your reaction to the speech? Be specific. . . . .

. . . .

. . . .

REPORT ON A SPEECH HEARD IN PUBLIC

Student's Name . . . . Class and Section . . . .

1. Name, title, and position of speaker: . . . .

. . . .

2. Subject: . . . .

3. Occasion: . . . .

4. Place: . . . . Time:. . . . . . Date: . . . .

5. Purpose of speech: to inform ☐ ;   to stimulate and arouse ☐ ;   to convince ☐ ; to get action ☐ ;   to entertain ☐ .

6. Explain the introduction and conclusion as to the type used. . . . .

. . . .

. . . .

7. What basic appeals did the speaker use? . . . .

. . . .

. . . .

8. Was the proof logical? emotional? personal? Explain. . . . .

. . . .

. . . .

9. Were sources of evidence stated accurately? Explain. . . . .

. . . .

. . . .

10. Describe the speaker's platform behavior. . . . .

. . . .

. . . .

11. Describe the speaker's use of language. . . . .

. . . .

. . . .

12. What was your reaction to the speech? Be specific. . . . .

. . . .

. . . .

(Use form on back for reporting another speech)

REPORT ON A SPEECH HEARD IN PUBLIC

Student's Name . . . . Class and Section . . . .

1. Name, title and position of speaker: . . . .

. . . .

2. Subject: . . . .

3. Occasion: . . . .

4. Place: . . . . Time: . . . . . . Date: . . . .

5. Purpose of speech: to inform ☐ ;   to stimulate and arouse ☐ ;   to convince ☐ ;
to get action ☐ ;   to entertain ☐ .

6. Explain the introduction and conclusion as to types used. . . . .

. . . .

. . . .

7. What basic appeals did the speaker use? . . . .

. . . .

. . . .

8. Was the proof logical? emotional? personal? Explain. . . . .

. . . .

. . . .

9. Were sources of evidence stated accurately? Explain. . . . .

. . . .

. . . .

10. Describe the speaker's platform behavior. . . . .

. . . .

. . . .

11. Describe the speaker's use of language. . . . .

. . . .

. . . .

12. What was your reaction to the speech? Be specific. . . . .

. . . .

. . . .

REPORT ON A SPEECH HEARD IN PUBLIC

Student's Name . . . . Class and Section . . . .

1. Name, title, and position of speaker: . . . .

. . . .

2. Subject: . . . .

3. Occasion: . . . .

4. Place: . . . . Time: . . . . . . Date: . . . .

5. Purpose of speech: to inform ☐ ;   to stimulate and arouse ☐ ;   to convince ☐ ;   to get action ☐ ;   to entertain ☐ .

6. Explain the introduction and conclusion as to the type used. . . . .

. . . .

. . . .

7. What basic appeals did the speaker use? . . . .

. . . .

. . . .

8. Was the proof logical? emotional? personal? Explain. . . . .

. . . .

. . . .

9. Were sources of evidence stated accurately? Explain. . . . .

. . . .

. . . .

10. Describe the speaker's platform behavior. . . . .

. . . .

. . . .

11. Describe the speaker's use of language. . . . .

. . . .

. . . .

12. What was your reaction to the speech? Be specific. . . . .

. . . .

. . . .

(Use form on back for reporting another speech)

REPORT ON A SPEECH HEARD IN PUBLIC

Student's Name ....Class and Section ....

1. Name, title and position of speaker:...
   ....

2. Subject: ....

3. Occasion: ....

4. Place: .... Time:...... Date: ....

5. Purpose of speech: to inform ☐ ;   to stimulate and arouse ☐ ;   to convince ☐ ;
   to get action ☐ ;   to entertain ☐ .

6. Explain the introduction and conclusion as to types used.......................................
   ....
   ....

7. What basic appeals did the speaker use?...
   ....
   ....

8. Was the proof logical? emotional? personal? Explain. ....
   ....
   ....

9. Were sources of evidence stated accurately? Explain..
   ....
   ....

10. Describe the speaker's platform behavior. ....
    ....
    ....

11. Describe the speaker's use of language. ....
    ....
    ....

12. What was your reaction to the speech? Be specific. ....
    ....
    ....

REPORT ON A SPEECH HEARD IN PUBLIC

Student's Name .... Class and Section ....

1. Name, title, and position of speaker: ....

....

2. Subject: ....

3. Occasion: ....

4. Place: .... Time:...... Date: ....

5. Purpose of speech: to inform ☐ ;   to stimulate and arouse ☐ ;   to convince ☐ ;
   to get action ☐ ;   to entertain ☐ .

6. Explain the introduction and conclusion as to the type used...................

....

....

7. What basic appeals did the speaker use?...............................

....

....

8. Was the proof logical? emotional? personal? Explain.....................

....

....

9. Were sources of evidence stated accurately? Explain. ....

....

....

10. Describe the speaker's platform behavior. ....

....

....

11. Describe the speaker's use of language. ....

....

....

12. What was your reaction to the speech? Be specific.....................

....

....

(Use form on back for reporting another speech)

REPORT ON A SPEECH HEARD IN PUBLIC

Student's Name ....Class and Section ....

1. Name, title and position of speaker: ....

   ....

2. Subject: ....

3. Occasion: ....

4. Place: .... Time: ......Date: ....

5. Purpose of speech: to inform ☐ ;   to stimulate and arouse ☐ ;   to convince ☐ ;
   to get action ☐ ;   to entertain ☐ .

6. Explain the introduction and conclusion as to types used. ....

   ....

   ....

7. What basic appeals did the speaker use? ....

   ....

   ....

8. Was the proof logical? emotional? personal? Explain. ....

   ....

   ....

9. Were sources of evidence stated accurately? Explain. ....

   ....

   ....

10. Describe the speaker's platform behavior. ....

    ....

    ....

11. Describe the speaker's use of language. ....

    ....

    ....

12. What was your reaction to the speech? Be specific. ....

    ....

    ....

STUDENT SPEECH CRITICISMS

One part of a speech course provides a student with an opportunity to listen to a speech and evaluate it. To criticize a speech is especially helpful because it makes one a more careful listener.

In using the forms which follow, the student critic should be fully aware that he is recording only his impressions of the speech. They will be governed by his physical comfort, his attentiveness, and his careful observation of all that he sees and hears. To be most valuable the impressions should be recorded with care and after some introspection into his own behavior while he was observing the speaker. Careless observation of a speaker produces at best no more than half valid criticism. In all fairness to the speaker the student critic should listen carefully and observe closely the points he is going to rate and comment on when he writes his impressions. By doing this he will increase the quality of his criticism and be of valuable help to the speaker.

- -

SPEECH CRITICISM

SPEAKER . . . .   SPEECH SUBJECT . . . .

Date . . . .   Critic's name . . . .

Write Comments

	Poor	Very weak	Weak	Fair	Adequate	Good	Very good	Excellent	Superior	
	1	2	3	4	5	6	7	8	9	
1. Introduction										. . . .
2. Clarity of purpose										. . . .
3. Language										. . . .
4. Bodily action, posture										. . . .
5. Eye contact, gestures										. . . .
6. Use of voice										. . . .
7. Enthusiasm, vigor										. . . .
8. Confidence, self-control										. . . .
9. Adaptation to audience										. . . .
10. Organization of material										. . . .
11. Conclusion										. . . .

SPEECH CRITICISM

SPEAKER. . . . .

Date . . . .

SPEECH SUBJECT. . . . .

Critic's name. . . . .

Write Comments

	Poor	Very weak	Weak	Fair	Adequate	Good	Very good	Excellent	Superior	
	1	2	3	4	5	6	7	8	9	
1. Introduction										. . . .
2. Clarity of purpose										. . . .
3. Language										. . . .
4. Bodily action, posture										. . . .
5. Eye contact, gestures										. . . .
6. Use of voice										. . . .
7. Enthusiasm, vigor										. . . .
8. Confidence, self-control										. . . .
9. Adaptation to audience										. . . .
10. Organization of material										. . . .
11. Conclusion										. . . .

- -

SPEECH CRITICISM

SPEAKER. . . . .

Date. . . . .

SPEECH SUBJECT. . . . .

Critic's name. . . . .

Write Comments

	Poor	Very weak	Weak	Fair	Adequate	Good	Very good	Excellent	Superior	
	1	2	3	4	5	6	7	8	9	
1. Introduction										. . . .
2. Clarity of purpose										. . . .
3. Language										. . . .
4. Bodily action, posture										. . . .
5. Eye contact, gestures										. . . .
6. Use of voice										. . . .
7. Enthusiasm, vigor										. . . .
8. Confidence, self-control										. . . .
9. Adaptation to audience										. . . .
10. Organization of material										. . . .
11. Conclusion										. . . .

SPEECH CRITICISM

SPEAKER . . . .   SPEECH SUBJECT . . . .

Date . . . .   Critic's name . . . .

	Poor	Very weak	Weak	Fair	Adequate	Good	Very good	Excellent	Superior	Write Comments
	1	2	3	4	5	6	7	8	9	
1. Introduction										. . . .
2. Clarity of purpose										. . . .
3. Language										. . . .
4. Bodily action, posture										. . . .
5. Eye contact, gestures										. . . .
6. Use of voice										. . . .
7. Enthusiasms, vigor										. . . .
8. Confidence, self-control										. . . .
9. Adaptation to audience										. . . .
10. Organization of material										. . . .
11. Conclusion										

- -

SPEECH CRITICISM

SPEAKER . . . .   SPEECH SUBJECT . . . .

Date . . . .   Critic's name . . . .

	Poor	Very weak	Weak	Fair	Adequate	Good	Very good	Excellent	Superior	Write Comments
	1	2	3	4	5	6	7	8	9	
1. Introduction										. . . .
2. Clarity of purpose										. . . .
3. Language										. . . .
4. Bodily action, posture										. . . .
5. Eye contact, gestures										. . . .
6. Use of voice										. . . .
7. Enthusiasm, vigor										. . . .
8. Confidence, self-control										. . . .
9. Adaptation to audience										. . . .
10. Organization of material										. . . .
11. Conclusion										

SPEECH OUTLINE

Name . . . . Date . . . . Type of speech . . . .

Specific purpose of this speech . . . .

. . . . No. of sources required . . . . .

Sentence outline: . . . . Time limit: . . . . Speaking notes: . . . .

TITLE

INTRODUCTION

BODY

CONCLUSION

INSTRUCTOR'S COMMENTS

Clarity of purpose . . . .

Gesture-action-eye contact . . . .

Language . . . .

Voice . . . .

Enthusiasm and vigor . . . .

Self-confidence . . . .

Organization . . . .

Introduction and conclusion . . . .

Grade . . . .

(List sources on back of page as indicated)

(179)

PRINTED SOURCES OF INFORMATION

Give complete information for each source.

1. Author's name ....
   Title of article ....
   Book or magazine containing article ....
   ....Date of publication ....
   Chapters and/or pages containing material ....

2. Author's name ....
   Title of article ....
   Book or magazine containing article ....
   ....Date of publication ....
   Chapters and/or pages containing material ....

3. Author's name ....
   Title of article ....
   Book or magazine containing article ....
   ....Date of publication ....
   Chapters and/or pages containing material ....

INTERVIEW SOURCES OF INFORMATION

1. Name of person interviewed...................Date of interview ....
   His title, position, and occupation ....
   ....
   Why is he an authority on the subject? Be specific ....
   ....

2. Name of person interviewed ....Date of interview ....
   His title, position, and occupation ....
   ....
   Why is he an authority on the subject? Be specific ....
   ....

3. Name of person interviewed ....Date of interview ....
   His title, position, and occupation ....
   ....
   Why is he an authority on the subject? Be specific ....
   ....

SPEECH OUTLINE

Name . . . . Date . . . . Type of speech . . . .

Specific purpose of this speech . . . .

. . . . No. of sources required . . . . .

Sentence outline: . . . . Time limit: . . . . Speaking notes: . . . .

TITLE

INTRODUCTION

BODY

CONCLUSION

INSTRUCTOR'S COMMENTS

   Clarity of purpose . . . .

   Gesture-action-eye contact . . . .

   Language . . . .

   Voice . . . .

   Enthusiasm and vigor . . . .

   Self-confidence . . . .

   Organization . . . .

   Introduction and conclusion . . . .

   Grade . . . .

(List sources on back of page as indicated)

PRINTED SOURCES OF INFORMATION

Give complete information for each source.

1. Author's name ....
   Title of article ....
   Book or magazine containing article ....
   ....Date of publication ....
   Chapters and/or pages containing material ....

2. Author's name ....
   Title of article ....
   Book or magazine containing article ....
   ....Date of publication ....
   Chapters and/or pages containing material ....

3. Author's name ....
   Title of article ....
   Book or magazine containing article ....
   ....Date of publication ....
   Chapters and/or pages containing material ....

INTERVIEW SOURCES OF INFORMATION

1. Name of person interviewed....................Date of interview ....
   His title, position, and occupation ....
   ....
   Why is he an authority on the subject? Be specific ....
   ....

2. Name of person interviewed ....Date of interview ....
   His title, position, and occupation ....
   ....
   Why is he an authority on the subject? Be specific ....
   ....

3. Name of person interviewed ....Date of interview ....
   His title, position, and occupation ....
   ....
   Why is he an authority on the subject? Be specific ....
   ....

SPEECH OUTLINE

Name . . . . Date . . . . Type of speech . . . .

Specific purpose of this speech . . . .

. . . . No. of sources required . . . . .

Sentence outline: . . . . Time limit: . . . . Speaking notes: . . . .

TITLF

INTRODUCTION

BODY

CONCLUSION

INSTRUCTOR'S COMMENTS

    Clarity of purpose . . . .

    Gesture-action-eye contact . . . .

    Language . . . .

    Voice . . . .

    Enthusiasm and vigor . . . .

    Self-confidence . . . .

    Organization . . . .

    Introduction and conclusion . . . .

    Grade . . . .

(List sources on back of page as indicated)

PRINTED SOURCES OF INFORMATION

Give complete information for each source.

1. Author's name ....
   Title of article ....
   Book or magazine containing article ....
   ....Date of publication ....
   Chapters and/or pages containing material ....

2. Author's name ....
   Title of article ....
   Book or magazine containing article ....
   ....Date of publication ....
   Chapters and/or pages containing material ....

3. Author's name ....
   Title of article ....
   Book or magazine containing article ....
   ....Date of publication ....
   Chapters and/or pages containing material ....

INTERVIEW SOURCES OF INFORMATION

1. Name of person interviewed..................Date of interview ......
   His title, position, and occupation ....
   ....
   Why is he an authority on the subject? Be specific ....
   ....

2. Name of person interviewed ....Date of interview ......
   His title, position, and occupation ....
   ....
   Why is he an authority on the subject? Be specific ....
   ....

3. Name of person interviewed ....Date of interview ......
   His title, position, and occupation ....
   ....
   Why is he an authority on the subject? Be specific ....
   ....

SPEECH OUTLINE

Name . . . . Date . . . . Type of speech . . . .

Specific purpose of this speech . . . .

. . . . No. of sources required . . . . .

Sentence outline: . . . . Time limit: . . . . Speaking notes: . . . .

TITLE

INTRODUCTION

BODY

CONCLUSION

INSTRUCTOR'S COMMENTS

Clarity of purpose . . . .

Gesture-action-eye contact . . . .

Language . . . .

Voice . . . .

Enthusiasm and vigor . . . .

Self-confidence . . . .

Organization . . . .

Introduction and conclusion . . . .

Grade . . . .

(List sources on back of page as indicated)

PRINTED SOURCES OF INFORMATION

Give complete information for each source.

1. Author's name . . . .
   Title of article . . . .
   Book or magazine containing article . . . .
   . . . . Date of publication . . . .
   Chapters and/or pages containing material . . . .
2. Author's name . . . .
   Title of article . . . .
   Book or magazine containing article . . . .
   . . . . Date of publication . . . .
   Chapters and/or pages containing material . . . .
3. Author's name . . . .
   Title of article . . . .
   Book or magazine containing article . . . .
   . . . . Date of publication . . . .
   Chapters and/or pages containing material . . . .

INTERVIEW SOURCES OF INFORMATION

1. Name of person interviewed . . . . Date of interview . . . .
   His title, position, and occupation . . . .
   . . . .
   Why is he an authority on the subject? Be specific . . . .
   . . . .
2. Name of person interviewed . . . . Date of interview . . . .
   His title, position, and occupation . . . .
   . . . .
   Why is he an authority on the subject? Be specific . . . .
   . . . .
3. Name of person interviewed . . . . Date of interview . . . .
   His title, position, and occupation . . . .
   . . . .
   Why is he an authority on the subject? Be specific . . . .
   . . . .

SPEECH OUTLINE

Name . . . . Date . . . . Type of speech . . . .

Specific purpose of this speech . . . .

. . . . No. of sources required . . . . .

Sentence outline: . . . . Time limit: . . . . Speaking notes: . . . .

TITLE

INTRODUCTION

BODY

CONCLUSION

INSTRUCTOR'S COMMENTS

Clarity of purpose . . . .

Gesture-action-eye contact . . . .

Language . . . .

Voice . . . .

Enthusiasm and vigor . . . .

Self-confidence . . . .

Organization . . . .

Introduction and conclusion . . . .

Grade . . . .

(List sources on back of page as indicated)

PRINTED SOURCES OF INFORMATION

Give complete information for each source.

1. Author's name ....
   Title of article ....
   Book or magazine containing article ....
   ....Date of publication ....
   Chapters and/or pages containing material ....

2. Author's name ....
   Title of article ....
   Book or magazine containing article ....
   ....Date of publication ....
   Chapters and/or pages containing material ....

3. Author's name ....
   Title of article ....
   Book or magazine containing article ....
   ....Date of publication ....
   Chapters and/or pages containing material ....

INTERVIEW SOURCES OF INFORMATION

1. Name of person interviewed...................Date of interview ....
   His title, position, and occupation ....
   ....
   Why is he an authority on the subject? Be specific ....
   ....

2. Name of person interviewed ....Date of interview ....
   His title, position, and occupation ....
   ....
   Why is he an authority on the subject? Be specific ....
   ....

3. Name of person interviewed ....Date of interview ....
   His title, position, and occupation ....
   ....
   Why is he an authority on the subject? Be specific ....
   ....

SPEECH OUTLINE

Name . . . . Date . . . . Type of speech . . . .

Specific purpose of this speech . . . .

. . . . No. of sources required . . . . .

Sentence outline: . . . . Time limit: . . . . Speaking notes: . . . .

TITLE

INTRODUCTION

BODY

CONCLUSION

INSTRUCTOR'S COMMENTS

    Clarity of purpose . . . .

    Gesture-action-eye contact . . . .

    Language . . . .

    Voice . . . .

    Enthusiasm and vigor . . . .

    Self-confidence . . . .

    Organization . . . .

    Introduction and conclusion . . . .

    Grade . . . .

(List sources on back of page as indicated)

PRINTED SOURCES OF INFORMATION

Give complete information for each source.

1. Author's name ....
   Title of article ....
   Book or magazine containing article ....
   ....Date of publication ....
   Chapters and/or pages containing material ....

2. Author's name ....
   Title of article ....
   Book or magazine containing article ....
   ....Date of publication ....
   Chapters and/or pages containing material ....

3. Author's name ....
   Title of article ....
   Book or magazine containing article ....
   ....Date of publication ....
   Chapters and/or pages containing material ....

INTERVIEW SOURCES OF INFORMATION

1. Name of person interviewed.................Date of interview ....
   His title, position, and occupation ....
   ....
   Why is he an authority on the subject? Be specific ....
   ....

2. Name of person interviewed ....Date of interview ....
   His title, position, and occupation ....
   ....
   Why is he an authority on the subject? Be specific ....
   ....

3. Name of person interviewed ....Date of interview ....
   His title, position, and occupation ....
   ....
   Why is he an authority on the subject? Be specific ....
   ....